Student V...

for

The Art of Public Speaking

Sixth Edition

Stephen E. Lucas
University of Wisconsin-Madison

Susan Zaeske
University of Wisconsin-Madison

McGraw-Hill College

Boston   Burr Ridge, IL   Dubuque, IA   Madison, WI   New York   San Francisco   St. Louis
Bangkok   Bogotá   Caracas   Lisbon   London   Madrid
Mexico City   Milan   New Delhi   Seoul   Singapore   Sydney   Taipei   Toronto

McGraw-Hill College

A Division of The McGraw·Hill Companies

Student Workbook for
THE ART OF PUBLIC SPEAKING

Copyright ©1998 by Stephen E. Lucas. All rights reserved.
Printed in the United States of America.

The contents of, or parts thereof, may be reproduced for use with
THE ART OF PUBLIC SPEAKING, by Stephen E. Lucas, provided such reproductions
bear copyright notice and may not be reproduced in any form for any other
purpose without permission of the publisher.

3 4 5 6 7 8 9 0 CUS/CUS 9 0 9

ISBN 0-07-043519-7

www.mhhe.com

TABLE OF CONTENTS

■ **Preface: A Message to the Student** — v

■ **Acknowledgments** — vi

■ **Welcome to Public Speaking**
- How to Succeed in Your Public Speaking Class — 1
- Introductory Questionnaire — 2
- Criteria Used for Evaluating Speeches — 3
- Student Responsibilities — 4

■ **The Introductory Speech**
- How to Give Your First Speech — 5
- Sample Speech of Self-Introduction — 13
- Tips for Using Narrative — 14
- Personal Report of Communication Apprehension — 15
- Tips for Dealing with Speech Anxiety — 16

■ **Ethics and Listening**
- Checklist for Ethical Public Speaking — 17
- Avoiding Plagiarism — 18
- Listening Self-Evaluation — 19
- Listening Worksheet — 20

■ **Topics, Purposes, and Audiences**
- Clustering Worksheet — 21
- Specific Purpose Checklist — 22
- Central Idea Checklist — 23
- Specific Purpose and Central Idea Exercises — 24
- Preparing an Audience-Analysis Questionnaire — 25
- Audience Analysis Worksheet — 26
- Audience Adaptation Worksheet — 27

■ **Gathering and Using Supporting Materials**
- Library Research Worksheet — 28
- Internet Research Worksheet — 29
- Supporting Materials Checklist — 30
- Supporting Materials Exercise — 31
- Bibliography Formats — 32

iii

■ Organizing and Outlining the Speech

Speech Organization Exercise	36
Main Points Checklist	37
Connectives Exercise	38
Speech Introduction Checklist	39
Speech Conclusion Checklist	40
Assessing Speech Introductions	41
Preparation Outline Guide	42
Preparation Outline Checklist	44
Scrambled Outline Exercise	45

■ Language, Delivery, and Visual Aids

Question-and-Answer Sessions	46
Tips for the Speaking Outline	47
Tips for Speaking from a Manuscript	48
Out-of-Class Speech Observation: Delivery	49
Checklist for Preparing Visual Aids	50
Checklist for Presenting Visual Aids	51

■ The Informative Speech

Informative Speech Topics	52
Informative Speech Preparation Worksheet	53
Informative Speech Self-Assessment	55

■ The Persuasive Speech

Persuasive Speech Topics	56
Fact, Value, or Policy?	57
Evidence Checklist	58
Persuasive Speech Preparation Worksheet	59
Reasoning Exercise	61
Speech Outline in Monroe's Motivated Sequence	62
Persuasive Speech Self-Assessment	64

■ The Special-Occasion Speech

Out-of-Class Observation for a Speech of Introduction	65
Special-Occasion Speech Self-Assessment	66

■ Small-Group Discussion

Reflective-Thinking Method Checklist	67
Group Discussion Self-Assessment	68

■ Speech Evaluation Forms

	71

PREFACE: A MESSAGE TO THE STUDENT

Welcome to your public speaking class. Although you may have enrolled in it to fulfill a requirement, you may find—as many students do—that it turns out to be your most enjoyable class of the term. Certainly it is one of the most important courses you will take in college. The skills you learn here—how to conduct research, how to organize the ideas you find in your research, how to support those ideas with evidence and reasoning, how to express yourself clearly and convincingly—will help you write term papers, make oral presentations, and compose essay exams in your other classes.

Those skills will also be invaluable in almost any career you choose. Whether you go into business, law, medicine, education, government, engineering, or community service, you will find that it is almost impossible to get ahead without strong communication skills. This is why many college graduates, in survey after survey, rank public speaking as the single most useful class of their college education. Students who enter the business world without strong public speaking skills often have to attend expensive seminars and workshops to acquire the skills they did not get in college. Your public speaking class teaches the same skills as these seminars and workshops—but at a fraction of the cost. You owe it to yourself to take full advantage of the class and the many benefits it can provide you.

Of course, none of these benefits can be acquired without work. Although many students enter their speech class thinking that it will be easy, they quickly discover that it requires a great deal of time and effort. As with most college courses, the more you put into your public speaking class, the more you will get out of it. Your instructor cannot make you become a better speaker. For that to happen, you must commit yourself to the course and be an active participant in it.

This workbook is designed to help you get the most out of your course. Written for use with your textbook, *The Art of Public Speaking*, sixth edition, it contains exercises, checklists, worksheets, and other materials that will help you master the principles of effective speechmaking presented in the book. At the end of the workbook, you will find evaluation forms that you can use when listening to the speeches of other students in class.

It is my hope that you will find your speech class to be a rewarding and enjoyable experience, and that this workbook will prove to be a valuable companion as you progress through *The Art of Public Speaking*.

Stephen E. Lucas
Madison, Wisconsin

ACKNOWLEDGMENTS

Page 4: "Student Responsibilities" is adapted, with permission of Karen P. Slawter, from course materials for Speech 101, Principles of Speech Communication, Northern Kentucky University.

Pages 5-12: "How to Give Your First Speech" is reprinted, with adaptations, from Carl R. Burgchardt, *How to Give Your First Speech: A Supplement to The Art of Public Speaking* (New York: McGraw-Hill, Inc., 1995).

Page 13: "You Are What You Eat" is printed with permission of Jennifer Fay.

Page 15: "Personal Report of Communication Apprehension (PRCA-24)" is reprinted with permission of James C. McCroskey.

Page 16: "Tips for Dealing with Speech Anxiety" is adapted, with permission of Vicki Abney Ragsdale, from course materials for Speech 101, Principles of Speech Communication, Northern Kentucky University.

Page 48: "Tips for Speaking from a Manuscript," is adapted from James A. Humes, *Talk Your Way to the Top* (New York: McGraw-Hill, 1980).

Pages 53-54: "Informative Speech Preparation Worksheet" is adapted, with permission of Kathy Kiser and Joyce Kuhn, from course materials for Speech and Drama 100, Fundamentals of Speech, Longview Community College.

Pages 62-63: "A Friend in Need" is adapted from Stephen E. Lucas, *The Art of Public Speaking*, 5th ed. (New York: McGraw-Hill, 1995).

HOW TO SUCCEED IN YOUR PUBLIC SPEAKING CLASS

1. **Strive for Perfect Attendance.** Every session of your speech class is designed to help you learn the material and master the skills of public speaking. Some days will be devoted to lecture, others to class discussion or activities, still others to the presentation of speeches by you and your classmates. You will learn something important every day—including the days on which you are listening to your classmates' speeches. The more faithfully you attend class, the better you will do in the course.

2. **Do the Assigned Readings and Do Them Ahead of Time.** Your textbook and other reading materials are designed to familiarize you with the principles of effective speechmaking. When you read the assigned material ahead of time, class discussion helps reinforce your understanding of what you have read in a way that doing the reading after class (or just before the exam) cannot.

3. **Learn the Language of Public Speaking.** Every area of study has its own specialized language. Terms such as *central idea*, *specific purpose*, *extemporaneous delivery*, *preparation outline*, and the like are part of the language of public speaking. Be sure you know what these terms mean.

4. **Participate in Class.** In addition to helping you learn the material better, class participation gives you more experience expressing your ideas in front of others. Most speech classes meet in small sections in which there is ample opportunity for discussion and sharing ideas. You owe it to yourself to take advantage of this opportunity.

5. **Ask Questions.** If you have no questions about the textbook, your speeches, or the class in general, you probably aren't putting much thought into the course. Asking questions is a good way to increase your understanding of the book, to help get ready for speeches, and to feel comfortable with your instructor and classmates.

6. **Spend Lots of Time Working on Your Speeches.** To get a sense of the time commitment required for this class, think of each major speech assignment as the equivalent of writing a paper in a composition class. The process of preparing a speech includes choosing a topic, narrowing the topic and settling on a specific purpose, researching the topic, determining the main points you will develop in the speech, writing an outline of the speech and organizing it so your ideas will come across clearly and convincingly, preparing visual aids to accompany the speech, and rehearsing the speech so you can deliver it fluently and confidently. Doing all of this well requires a great deal of effort. The more time you spend working on your speeches, the better they will be. Many B speeches could become A's with a little more work.

7. **Begin Working on Your Speeches Well in Advance.** Because it takes a lot of time to prepare an effective speech, it is vital that you begin working on your speeches as soon as they are assigned. This way you will be able to spend the night before your presentation fine-tuning your delivery rather than racing feverishly to prepare the content of your remarks. In addition to giving you plenty of time to work through all the stages of speech preparation, getting an early start will help you avoid the dangers of plagiarism that arise when students leave all of their speech preparation to the last minute.

8. **Get Feedback on Your Speeches.** Get feedback from your teacher. Most instructors are willing to look at several drafts of a speech and to make suggestions for improvement. You can also get feedback from family, friends, roommates, and classmates. They may not be able to give as much advice as your instructor, but they can tell you if you are saying "um" or looking down at your notes too often. Whatever you do, take advantage of feedback that can help you become a better, more confident speaker.

INTRODUCTORY QUESTIONNAIRE

Name _____ Year in School _____

Major _____

Are you taking this class as a requirement or an elective? If you are taking it to fulfill a requirement, what requirement is it fulfilling?

What kinds of speaking experiences have you had in classes, jobs, extracurricular activities, organizations, etc.?

What are your career plans? Will public speaking be important to your career? How so?

What do you believe are your greatest strengths as a public speaker? Be specific.

What are your goals for improving your public speaking in this course? Be specific.

CRITERIA USED FOR EVALUATING SPEECHES

The *average speech* (grade C) should meet the following criteria:

1. Conform to the kind of speech assigned (informative, persuasive, etc.)
2. Be ready for presentation on the assigned date
3. Conform to the time limit
4. Fulfill any special requirements of the assignment such as preparing an outline, using visual aids, conducting an interview, etc.
5. Have a clear specific purpose and central idea
6. Have an identifiable introduction, body, and conclusion
7. Show reasonable directness and competence in delivery
8. Be free of serious errors in grammar, pronunciation, and word usage

The *above average speech* (grade B) should meet the preceding criteria and also:

1. Deal with a challenging topic
2. Fulfill all major functions of a speech introduction and conclusion
3. Display clear organization of main points and supporting materials
4. Support main points with evidence that meets the tests of accuracy, relevance, objectivity, and sufficiency
5. Exhibit proficient use of connectives—transitions, internal previews, internal summaries, and signposts
6. Be delivered skillfully enough so as not to distract attention from the speaker's message

The *superior speech* (grade A) should meet all the preceding criteria and also:

1. Constitute a genuine contribution by the speaker to the knowledge or beliefs of the audience
2. Sustain positive interest, feeling, and/or commitment among the audience
3. Contain elements of vividness and special interest in the use of language
4. Be delivered in a fluent, polished manner that strengthens the impact of the speaker's message

The *below average speech* (grade D or F) is seriously deficient in the criteria required for the C speech.

STUDENT RESPONSIBILITIES

1. Arrive on time for class. Arriving late is distracting and disruptive.

2. If you arrive late during a speech, do not enter the classroom. Wait by the door and enter only after you hear applause at the end of the speech.

3. Listen attentively to the speeches of your classmates. Do not read the newspaper, talk with other students, or stare idly out the window during a speech. Show your classmates the same courtesy and attention you expect from them when you are speaking.

4. Put away all items such as personal stereos, homework, magazines, textbooks, and the like when speeches are in progress.

5. Refrain from asking questions until the end of a speech.

6. Turn in speech outlines and all other written work on the day it is due. Do not assume that late work will be accepted.

7. If you must miss a class, it is your responsibility to get all handouts, notes, and assignments from that day.

8. Be in class without fail on days when you are assigned to speak. Being absent will throw off the speaking schedule and may well result in a major penalty on your grade.

9. If you become ill and will have to miss several classes, notify your instructor immediately. Be prepared to document your illness.

10. If you cannot meet with your instructor during posted office hours, make—and keep—an appointment to meet with her or him at another time.

HOW TO GIVE YOUR FIRST SPEECH

The most important step in becoming an effective public speaker is to gain experience giving speeches. As early as the first day of class, your instructor will probably announce that everyone will soon be presenting a short speech. You are probably thinking, "What am I supposed to do? I have barely started this course, yet the teacher wants me to stand up in front of my classmates and talk! I don't have any speaking experience; I haven't read more than a few pages in the textbook; and I don't have the foggiest notion how to begin!"

If these are your thoughts, you are not alone. Most beginning speech students have precisely the same reaction. Fortunately, giving your first speech sounds a lot harder than it is. The next few pages will provide the information you need to do a good job on this assignment: how to select a topic, how to focus your speech, how to make your speech more interesting, how to organize your speech, how to prepare and practice your speech, how to behave during the presentation, and how to cope with stage fright.

WHY DO THIS ASSIGNMENT?

Many public speaking instructors ask students to give a short, simple icebreaker speech very early in the course. As its name implies, the purpose of this speech is to "break the ice" by getting students up in front of the class as soon as possible. Instructors know from experience that much of the anxiety associated with public speaking comes from lack of experience in giving speeches. Once students have broken the ice by giving a speech, they feel less anxious and begin to develop sound public speaking habits that lead to confidence.

In some classes this initial assignment is called a diagnostic speech because the instructor will use it to diagnose your strengths and weaknesses. Your teacher will then have a better idea of how to help you become a more effective speaker. Still other classes label this assignment an introductory speech because its purpose is to introduce yourself or a classmate to the audience and, in the process, give you an introduction to the art of public speaking.

Regardless of what the first assignment is called, its goal is to give you valuable public speaking experience in a low-pressure, supportive setting. It is also a good way for you to meet your classmates and begin to learn who they are. The more familiar you become with your classmates, the more comfortable you will feel the next time you give a speech to them.

HOW DO I SELECT A TOPIC?

Your instructor probably will give you a clear explanation that specifies the kind of topic you should select. For your initial presentation, many teachers prefer an exercise in which students break into pairs, interview each other, and, on the day of the speech, introduce the other person to the class with a short biographical talk. Other teachers assign a speech of self-introduction in which each student introduces himself or herself to the class. One approach to this speech is to have students go to the library and read through a newspaper from the day they were born or a magazine such as *Time* or *Newsweek* from the week they were born. Students then select an item—article, advertisement, photograph, editorial, etc.—from the newspaper or magazine that relates to the speaker's life in some significant way. Using that item as a point of departure, the student constructs a speech that explains some aspect of her or his personality, background, beliefs, or aspirations.

There are many other approaches to the speech of self-introduction. One is an assignment in which students speak on a significant aspect of their cultural background and how it has made a difference in their lives. Possible topics include social customs, family traditions, holidays, clothing, food, religious beliefs, sporting activities, and the like. Another possibility is the "Brush with Greatness" speech in which students explain how they met a celebrity or visited a famous place. As an alternative, you might be asked to give a speech titled "My Pet Peeve," in which you explain something that particularly annoys you—bad drivers, obnoxious roommates, phone solicitations, etc. Or, in a more positive vein, you might give a speech about a personal object of special significance, such as a cherished book, a musical instrument, or a photograph. All of these assignments, like those discussed in the previous paragraph, are designed to give the audience insight into your background, outlook, personality, and goals.

No matter what the assignment for your initial speech, do your best to understand precisely what your teacher requires. In order to do well in the course, you must fulfill the speaking assignments exactly. If something is unclear about the expectations for your speech, be sure to ask for clarification.

HOW DO I FOCUS MY SPEECH?

Whether your instructor assigns a specific topic or provides a number of options, you will need to gather material to include in your talk. After you have settled on a particular subject, be certain the focus of your speech is narrow enough to conform to the time limit. One of the most common mistakes students make on their first speech is to try to cover too much material. Not only does this cause your speech to go over the time limit, but it results in content that is too general or superficial. So you should select a limited amount of focused material that is illustrated thoroughly.

For example, you cannot give a tightly focused speech about "music" in a two- or three-minute presentation. There are simply too many facets to this subject. A better idea would be to give a speech on "My Most Unusual Experiences as a Member of the Marching Band." This allows you to make a few well-developed points about a clearly defined subject. On the other hand, avoid the temptation to narrow the focus of your topic too much. Few listeners would be pleased to hear a two- or three-minute discussion of advanced trumpet-playing techniques. Such a speech would be too specialized for most classroom audiences.

HOW CAN I MAKE MY SPEECH INTERESTING?

You should strive to make your introductory speech as creative and interesting as possible. But how do you select material that will please the audience? We know from experience that certain general traits tend to make a compelling speech. While your talk need not include all of these traits, it would be helpful if it incorporated some of them.

First, think of ways to make your speech mysterious or suspenseful. Radio commentator Paul Harvey has mastered the technique of telling a fascinating story about the accomplishments of an important individual but not revealing the identity of that person until the very end. Motorists who listen to these tales on their car radios are frequently unwilling to leave their vehicles until the mystery person is named. Such a technique could easily be applied in your first public speaking assignment. If you were telling the audience about your brush with greatness, for example, consider withholding the identity of your celebrity until the end. As your story unfolds, tantalize your classmates with clues about your celebrity's gender, physical characteristics, special talents, and the like, but keep the name a secret until the last moment. The idea is to hold your classmates on the edges of their seats as they listen.

In addition to mystery and suspense, audiences are naturally interested in dangerous situations, adventure, and drama. If your task is to introduce a fellow student, for instance, find out if he or she has ever been in danger. Suppose your classmate went on a whitewater rafting expedition and fell overboard. The story of how this person was rescued would be very dramatic. Or perhaps last summer you worked as a counselor in a crisis intervention center. The details of such a job might make excellent material for a speech of self-introduction. If you think about it, every person has faced risk, done the unusual, or triumphed over hardship. Try to find ways to include such fascinating experiences in your speech.

Another way to make a speech interesting is to use colorful, descriptive language that appeals to your audience's senses. If you were giving a "Pet Peeve" speech about your messy roommate, for instance, go beyond the general statement that "My roommate never washes the dishes." Describe the mountains of filthy plates that teeter in the sink; delve into the details of dried-out gravy welded to the dishes. Or suppose you are speaking about a cherished object—say your dog, Kuma. Make your speech come alive by vividly describing how Kuma wags his tail when he is excited, or how he rests his head on your knee when you are watching television. Colorful and concrete illustrations are invariably more interesting in a speech than dull language and abstract generalizations.

Students often ask about using humor to make their speeches more interesting. Audiences love witty remarks, jokes, and funny situations, but humor is only effective when done well. It should flow naturally out of the content of the speech, rather than being contrived. If you are not normally a funny person, you are better off giving a sincere, enthusiastic speech and leaving the jokes out. All speakers should refrain from humor that is tasteless or not directly relevant to the topic. It almost goes without saying that you should avoid jokes that embarrass specific individuals or negatively stereotype groups of people. The best kind of humor pokes fun at ourselves or at universal human foibles. Everyone in the audience will be able to enjoy that kind of humor.

HOW SHOULD I ORGANIZE MY SPEECH?

Some speeches seem to organize themselves. If your instructor asks you to tell a story of your brush with greatness, you will relate what happened when you met a celebrity or visited a famous place. The basic structure for such a speech is chronological: "This happened; then this happened; then this happened."

Speeches that tell a story are excellent ways of giving students experience talking in front of the class, but not all speeches follow this format. Suppose your instructor asks you to give a two-minute presentation introducing one of your classmates. You could organize the most important biographical facts about your subject in chronological order, but this might result in a dry, superficial speech: "In 1976 Alicia was born in Cleveland, attended Garfield Elementary School from 1982 to 1988, and graduated from Hoover High School in 1994." A better way of structuring your remarks might be to discuss three of the most important aspects of Alicia's life, such as hobbies, career goals, and family. This is called the topical method of organization, which subdivides the speech topic into its natural, logical, or conventional parts. Although there are many other ways to organize a speech, your first presentation will probably use either chronological or topical order.

Regardless of the subject, your speech will have three main parts—an introduction, a body, and a conclusion. What should a good introduction do? First, it needs to engage the attention and interest of the audience. You can attract your classmates' attention simply by walking to the front of the room and beginning to speak in a loud voice. The hard part is arousing their interest. Your first few sentences are vitally important. There are many methods you can use in the opening lines of a speech to engage the interest of your audience. You can tell a story, state the significance of your topic, open with a quotation, pose a question, present a startling fact or statistic, or relate how the topic affects the audience directly. The purpose of all these methods is to create a dramatic, colorful opening that will make your audience want to hear more.

If you were giving a "Brush with Greatness" speech about your encounter with television talk-show host Oprah Winfrey, you might begin like this:

> Who is the highest-paid female entertainer on television? Who did *Time* magazine rank as the most respected talk-show host? Who can make or break a book simply by featuring it on her televised book club? Who has quietly donated millions of dollars to charities and other worthy causes? If you answered "Oprah Winfrey" to any of these questions, you would be absolutely correct.

By opening with a series of questions, you arouse the curiosity of the audience and get them interested in your speech. Moreover, as you move from question to question, some audience members will figure out the answer. They may begin smiling and nodding their heads knowingly.

In addition to gaining attention and interest, the introduction should orient your audience toward the subject matter of your speech. In the example just mentioned, we move quickly from the opening questions to a sharp focus on Oprah Winfrey. In longer speeches, your introduction might need to add some brief background information or define key terms, but your first speech will probably not need to do either.

Near the end of the introduction, you should clearly state the specific purpose of your speech. In the "Brush with Greatness" speech you might say, "Today I will explain my brush with greatness that occurred last summer when I was a guest on the Oprah Winfrey show." Immediately after announcing your specific purpose, you should provide your audience with a "road map" for the rest of your speech by previewing or forecasting the major points. In the "Brush with Greatness" speech you could say something like, "I will discuss how I got invited to appear on the Oprah show, my experiences on the show, and my impressions of Oprah herself." Once you have completed these steps, it's time to move on to the body of your speech.

The body should follow a distinct organizational format such as chronological or topical. In your first speech, usually all you need to worry about is keeping your major ideas related to each other and clearly focused. The main points should directly illustrate or explain the overall topic, yet each point should develop different aspects of it. Suppose you were introducing a classmate. All of your points should provide interesting biographical information about that person. Relevant subjects might include his or her family, relationships, academic major, home town, hopes for the future, special talents, preferred food, favorite music, job, hobbies, and the like.

Remember to limit the number of main points. If your speech has too many main points, your audience will struggle to recognize the most important ideas. In a two-minute speech, you probably won't have time to develop more than two or three main points. Once you have selected those points, make sure each one focuses on a single aspect of the topic. For example, if your first point concerns your classmate's home town, don't introduce irrelevant information about her job or favorite music. Save this material for a separate point, or cut it from the speech altogether.

Try to make the structure of the body stand out by introducing each main point with a transition statement. In a hypothetical speech of introduction, you might begin the first main point by saying: "Megan grew up on a farm in the southern part of the state." The second point might commence along these lines: "Living and working on a farm led to Megan's great love of animals, especially horses. In fact, her favorite hobby is Western-style horseback riding." You have now let your audience know that the first main point is over and that you are starting the second one. The third main point might begin as follows: "Horseback riding is more than just a hobby for Megan. Her academic major at the university is equine science, which concerns the care, management, and business of horses." When you have completed your final point, you are ready to move to the conclusion.

In the conclusion, you will need to accomplish two tasks. First, let your audience know you are about to finish your speech. Second, review the main points. If possible, try to end on a dramatic, funny, or thought-provoking note. Suppose you are giving a speech about national events on the day you were born. You might finish like this: "In conclusion, a lot of bad things happened on July 23, 1970. In a single day, our country suffered a flood, a forest fire, and an earthquake. I hope you can see why some people consider my birthday a national disaster!" Such an ending ties up the presentation and allows the speaker to finish on a strong note.

HOW SHOULD I PREPARE MY SPEECH FOR DELIVERY?

Once you have selected an appropriate subject and organized the content into a clear structure, it is time to prepare your speech for delivery. A common impulse of many students is to write out their speech like an essay and to read it word for word to their listeners. The other extreme is to prepare very little for the speech—to wing it by trusting to your wits and the inspiration of the moment. Neither approach, however, is appropriate for your introductory talk. Reading your speech from a manuscript runs the risk of poor eye contact with the audience and a stiff, unenthusiastic delivery. On the other hand, ad-libbing the speech is a recipe for disaster. The outcome is usually a rambling, disorganized talk that is embarrassingly short.

The best approach for your first speech is called the extemporaneous method, which combines the careful preparation and structure of a manuscript presentation with the spontaneity and enthusiasm of an unrehearsed talk. Your aim in an extemporaneous speech is to plan out your major points and supporting material without trying to memorize the precise language you will use on the day of the speech.

The extemporaneous method requires you to know the content of your speech quite well. In fact, when you use the extemporaneous method properly, you become so familiar with the substance of your talk that you need only some brief notes to remind you of the points you intend to cover. The notes should consist only of key words or phrases that jog your memory, rather than of complete sentences or paragraphs. This way, when you stand up in front of the audience, you will tell them what you know about your topic in your own words.

Prepare your notes by writing or printing key terms and phrases on index cards or sheets of paper. Some instructors require students to use index cards because they are small and unobtrusive, don't rustle or flop over, and can be held in one hand, which allows the speaker to gesture more easily. Other teachers recommend sheets of paper because you can get more information on them, there are fewer objects to handle, and it is easier to print out computer files on paper. If you are unsure what your instructor prefers, be sure to ask well before your speech is due.

Whether you use index cards or sheets of paper, your notes should be large enough to see clearly at arm's length. Many experienced speakers prefer to double or triple space their notes because this makes it easier to see the notes during the speech. Write or print only on one side of the sheet of paper or index card, so you don't have to flip it over before moving on to the next one. Number your notes in case you accidentally drop them. Finally, use the fewest notes that you can manage and still present the speech fluently and confidently.

At first the extemporaneous method may seem very demanding, but when you think about it, you will recognize that you use aspects of this method all the time in your personal conversations with friends. Do you read from a manuscript when you tell your friends an amusing story or relate the events of a date or a trip? Of course not. You recall the essential details of your story, and you tell the tale to different friends on different occasions using somewhat different language each time. You feel relaxed and confident with your friends, so you just tell them what is on your mind in a conversational tone. You should try to do the same thing in your first speech.

HOW SHOULD I PRACTICE MY SPEECH?

Delivering a speech extemporaneously calls for significant practice to get it right. Because most of the speeches you will give in your public speaking course require the extemporaneous method, you should make a concerted effort to use it well in your introductory assignment. When you become truly proficient at extemporaneous speaking, your audiences will be amazed at your excellent eye contact and sincere, spontaneous delivery. But, of course, you need to practice in the proper way. The first time you rehearse your speech, you will probably struggle. Words may not come to you easily, and you might forget some things you planned to say. Don't become discouraged. Every time you practice, it will get easier.

Rehearse the speech in a loud voice. This is more inconvenient than silently looking over your notes, but the physical process of speaking the words out loud will aid you in mastering the content of your talk. Once you have a fairly good grasp on the speech, practice in the presence of other people and ask for their reactions. You will get a much better sense of how well you know the speech if you can deliver it to friends or family members. Giving the speech to a live audience when you practice will also make it easier to present it later in class.

As you practice, time your presentation with a stopwatch or clock. Most instructors enforce strict time limits on speeches. Be sure you understand the minimum and maximum times allowed for your presentation. Because of nerves, most people talk faster during their first speech than when they practice it. When you rehearse at home, make certain your speech runs slightly longer than the minimum time limit. That way, if your speaking rate increases when you present the speech in class, you will not end up with a speech that is too short. Don't be surprised, however, if the timing of your speech varies somewhat as you practice. It would be a bad sign if your speech took *exactly* the same amount of time during each rehearsal, because that would indicate that you were reading from a manuscript or had memorized the speech verbatim.

HOW SHOULD I BEHAVE DURING MY SPEECH?

When it is your turn to speak, move to the front of the room and face the audience. Assume a relaxed but upright posture. If you are standing, plant your feet a bit less than shoulder width apart. Allow your arms to hang loosely by your side or in front of your body. Before beginning your speech, carefully arrange your notes. Then take a moment to look over your audience and to smile. This will being to establish rapport with your classmates from the start.

Once you are into the speech, feel free to use your hands to gesture, but don't worry overly about planning your gestures ahead of time. If you are not a person who ordinarily uses your hands or body expressively during informal conversation, then don't try to fake it while speaking in public. It is particularly important during your first speech to allow your hand gestures and facial expressions to flow naturally and spontaneously from your feelings.

You should do your best to avoid nervous mannerisms such as twisting your hair, wringing your hands, shifting your weight from one foot to the other, rocking back and forth, tapping your fingers on the lectern, or jingling coins in your pockets. No matter how nervous you feel, try to appear calm and relaxed. Your instructor does not expect a flawless performance. If you have some nervous habits, she or he will help you identify them and suggest remedies for later speeches.

During your talk, try to look at your classmates as often as you can. One of the major reasons for speaking extemporaneously is to maintain eye contact with your audience. You know, from your own experience, how much more impressive a speaker is when she or he looks at the audience while speaking. If you have practiced the extemporaneous method of delivery and prepared your notes properly, you ought to be able to maintain eye contact with your audience most of the time. In a small public speaking class, try to look briefly and evenly at each person as the speech progresses. Be sure to look to the left and right of the room, as well as the center, and avoid the temptation to speak exclusively to one or two sympathetic individuals. When you are finished speaking, your classmates should have the impression that you tried to use your eyes to establish a personal connection with each of them.

Beginning speech students typically make three kinds of mistakes with their voice: they speak too softly, they speak too quickly, and they do not pronounce their words distinctly. Therefore, the most important elements of voice that you should practice for your first speech are loudness, rate, and articulation. If you do well on these, most other aspects of vocal delivery will fall into place.

For your first speech, concentrate on projecting your voice to the back of the room. Unless you see your audience cringing and covering their ears, you will probably not be too loud. Second, fight the temptation to race through your speech. Speak slowly enough that your audience can comfortably comprehend your sentences. Third, try to articulate each word clearly, but don't overenunciate, which might make you sound snobbish or odd. If you make a conscious effort to speak up, slow down, and speak clearly, you are on the right track to an effective presentation.

WHAT ABOUT STAGE FRIGHT?

Although we don't feel nervous conversing with our friends in private, many of us are anxious about giving a formal speech to a group of strangers in an unfamiliar situation. Most students experience stage fright before giving their first speeches. This is entirely normal. You can be sure that your fellow students share the same fears. In fact, one way you can help your classmates with their nervousness is by being a friendly, receptive listener. When others are speaking, look at them, smile and nod encouragingly, laugh at their jokes, and, in general, show that you are interested in what they are saying. When it is your chance to speak, you will appreciate similar behavior in return.

As your speech class progresses, you will get to know your classmates better, and you will become increasingly comfortable addressing them. As you complete your public speaking assignments with success, your confidence will grow. If you are like most students, by the end of the class you will feel considerably less anxious about speaking in public.

You are probably thinking, "All of that is fine for the future, but what about now?" First of all, realize that a certain amount of stage fright is actually a good thing. Many actors, musicians, and athletes believe that nervous energy enhances their level of performance. In fact, there are many stories of such people performing poorly on occasions when they are not nervous. The more experience you gain as a speaker, the easier it will be for you to use your nervousness to give an energetic, enthusiastic, animated speech.

Even then, however, you may still feel unpleasant physical symptoms on the day of your speech. Sweaty hands, dry mouth, blushing, dizziness, and upset stomach are some typical symptoms of speech anxiety. Fortunately, most of these symptoms will subside once you are into your speech.

In addition, you are likely to be in better physical condition for speaking if you follow a few commonsense tips. Get plenty of rest the night before the speech. Avoid dehydration by drinking water throughout the day of your presentation. If possible, try to eat a solid meal a few hours before class. If you have butterflies in your stomach before delivering your speech, sit quietly in your chair and take several slow, deep breaths. This will relax you and reduce your discomfort by getting more oxygen to your brain. The best advice for stemming stage fright has already been discussed—practice, practice, practice. Rehearsing your speech the proper way is the single most effective way to build confidence and to combat stage fright.

CONCLUSION

By now you should have the basic information you need to make your first speech a positive experience. All of the topics discussed here are developed in much more detail in your textbook. As your public speaking class unfolds, you will gain a more sophisticated understanding of the communication process. For now, keep your introductory assignment in perspective. Remember that your instructor does not expect perfection. You are not a professional speaker, and this is the first speech of the class. Do your best on the assignment, but don't be afraid to have fun with it. One purpose of this speech is to help your instructor and classmates learn more about you, so let your personality shine through. Plan what you want to say, organize the material clearly, practice thoroughly, and use the extemporaneous method of delivery. You may be surprised by how much you enjoy giving your first speech.

SAMPLE SPEECH OF SELF-INTRODUCTION

YOU ARE WHAT YOU EAT
Jennifer Fay

You are all familiar with the phrase, "You are what you eat." To most of you, this phrase is no more than a silly cliché your grandmother used to get you to eat healthy foods like buttered whole-wheat toast or Jell-O with fruit in it. For me, this phrase has been a way of life for two reasons. The first reason is that my mother reared me to eat healthy food. The second reason is that my mother instilled in me the notion that I am no greater than the sum of my meal. Since my mother's conception of healthy food changed drastically over the course of my childhood, I stand before you today a much different person than I was twenty-nine years ago. In the next few minutes, I want to tell you about who I was and who I am through what I've eaten.

It's fitting that on the day I was born, April 4th, 1969, McDonald's premiered its new culinary invention, the Big Mac, in the April issue of *Life* magazine. The ad read, "It's a meal disguised as a sandwich." In a manner of speaking, a Big Mac was a whole meal because it contained at least one item from each of the four major food groups. My mother was an advocate of the square meal, and the Big Mac fit the bill. The Big Mac had cheese and special sauce from the dairy group, plus tomato, pickle and lettuce from the fruit and vegetable group. It had bread from the cereal and grains group and beef from the meat group. Even pizza was healthy under the square meal plan. This plan was the early phase of my selfhood—fast, frozen foods that were easy to make and supposedly good for you. No surprises, no rules. My friends liked to have dinner at my house.

One morning my mother became conscious of her weight and changed our diet to Weight Watchers' fare. Food was still fast and frozen, but it was low-cal and in smaller amounts. Four ounces of tuna and one slice of processed cheese—this was dinner. A single scoop of ice milk was dessert. My mother and I were hungry, but she felt that suffering was good for the soul.

The diet phase did not stop with Weight Watchers. One diet led to another as entire food groups dropped from our meal plan. By the time I was in high school, I found myself living in a macrobiotic nightmare. My mother renounced the Big Mac and pizza forever. She said they were harmful and, in large amounts, even toxic.

It was during this macrobiotic phase that our cupboards were filled with foods I could not identify; on our plates were entrées I could not pronounce. I was now fat-free, salt-free, sugar-free, meat-free and dairy-free. With frightening tenacity, my mother clung to the maxim, "You are what you eat." If I was sad, she'd accuse me of eating cheese at a friend's house. If I was mad, she'd tell me to lay off the acidic fruits and vegetables. During this phase of my life, food preparation was long and eating was joyless. Friends stopped coming over for dinner and I longed to be free from the burden of hunger.

I finally went away to school where I reacquainted myself with the fast, frozen, fun foods of my youth—sugar cereals, pizza, Tater Tots and, yes, Big Macs. My mother hardly recognized me when I came home that first semester. "You've changed your diet," she sighed. This gluttonous phase lasted through my junior year when I realized that I would soon have a weight problem of my own. I knew that I must find a meal plan that was all mine.

I am proud to say that today I stand before you, twenty-nine years after the introduction of the Big Mac, not as a Big Mac, though Big Macs I have ordered, not as a block of tofu, though tofu I have prepared, but as a happy balance of pasta and wine, cereal and coffee, sandwiches and soda. That's what I've eaten and that's what I am.

TIPS FOR USING NARRATIVE

Narratives are stories that are used to convey a lesson or a to illustrate a point. They may be real or hypothetical, brief or extended. Some narratives are based on a speaker's personal experience, others on historical events, still others on myths or fables. Narratives are important to public speakers because they translate abstract concepts into personal stories with characters, plot, conflict, and resolution. When delivered effectively, such stories pull listeners into a speech and allow the speaker to convey his or her ideas with great effectiveness. In some cultures, public speeches often revolve entirely around a lengthy narrative or a series of shorter narratives.

Depending on your speech class, you may be asked to deliver a brief narrative speech early in the term. The speech may be one in which you introduce yourself to the class, or it may be one in which you introduce a classmate. In either case, you may find yourself using narrative to explain a significant aspect of your—or your classmate's—life, culture, background, or personality. For an excellent example of such a speech, see "You Are What You Eat," the sample introductory speech on page 13 of this workbook.

Although "You Are What You Eat" is an introductory speech, you can also use narratives in informative, persuasive, and commemorative addresses. As you read through your textbook, you will find many excellent examples of narratives in student presentations, including "Dying to Be Thin," an informative speech on pages A11-A13, "The Dangers of Chewing Tobacco," a persuasive speech on pages 429-432, and "Questions of Culture," a commemorative speech on pages A2-A4.

No matter what kind of speech you are presenting, there are several steps you can take to use narrative effectively.

1. Make your narrative clear and easy to follow. In most cases, it should be organized chronologically. Include transitions and other markers that will let your audience know when the narrative is shifting in time or place.

2. Be certain your narrative makes sense and answers all the questions it raises. For example, in a speech about financial aid, don't leave the audience wondering what happened to a character who was concerned about getting enough money to attend college. As with any good story, your narrative should be complete and coherent.

3. Make your narrative vivid and richly textured. Notice how the speaker provides a wealth of specific details throughout "You Are What You Eat." These details bring the narrative to life and make it interesting to listeners. Try to do the same in your speeches.

4. If you are using a hypothetical narrative—one that did not really occur—be sure to tell the audience that the story is imaginary.

5. Rehearse your narrative so you can deliver it without being tied to your speaking notes. No matter how gripping a story might be in written form, it will fall flat with listeners unless it is presented with strong eye contact and in a lively, expressive voice. Speak faster here to create a sense of action, slower there to build suspense. Raise your voice at some places and lower it in others. Pause occasionally for dramatic effect. Try to tell your story as naturally and confidently as if you were relating it to a group of friends.

PERSONAL REPORT OF COMMUNICATION APPREHENSION
(PRCA-24)

This questionnaire is composed of 24 statements concerning feelings about communicating with other people. Please indicate the degree to which each statement applies to you by marking whether you (1) strongly agree, (2) agree, (3) are undecided, (4) disagree, or (5) strongly disagree. Work quickly; record your first reaction.

1. Generally, I am comfortable while participating in group discussions.
2. While participating in a conversation with a new acquaintance, I feel very nervous.
3. I am very relaxed when answering questions at a meeting.
4. My thoughts become confused and jumbled while I am giving a speech.
5. I am tense and nervous while participating in group discussions.
6. Ordinarily I am very calm and relaxed in conversations.
7. I am afraid to express myself at meetings.
8. I face the prospect of giving a speech with confidence.
9. I like to get involved in group discussions.
10. Ordinarily I am very tense and nervous in conversations.
11. Communicating at meetings usually makes me uncomfortable.
12. I feel relaxed while giving a speech.
13. Engaging in a group discussion with new people makes me tense and nervous.
14. I have no fear of speaking up in conversations.
15. I am very calm and relaxed when I am called upon to express an opinion at a meeting.
16. Certain parts of my body feel very tense and rigid while I am giving a speech.
17. I am calm and relaxed while participating in group discussions.
18. I'm afraid to speak up in conversations.
19. Generally, I am nervous when I have to participate in a meeting.
20. I have no fear of giving a speech.
21. I dislike participating in group discussions.
22. While conversing with a new acquaintance, I feel very relaxed.
23. Usually I am calm and relaxed while participating in meetings.
24. While giving a speech, I get so nervous that I forget facts I really know.

SCORING: The questionnaire allows you to compute one total score and four subscores. The subscores are related to communication apprehension in four common communication contexts: group discussions, interpersonal conversations, meetings, and public speaking. To compute your scores, add or subtract your answers for each item as indicated below:

Subscore Desired	*Scoring Formula*
Group Discussions	18 plus scores for items 1, 9, and 17; minus scores for items 5, 13, and 21
Interpersonal Conversations	18 plus scores for items 6, 14, and 22; minus scores for items 2, 10, and 18
Meetings	18 plus scores for items 3, 15, and 23; minus scores for items 7, 11, and 19
Public Speaking	18 plus scores for items 8, 12, and 20; minus scores for items 4, 16, and 24

To obtain your total score for the PRCA, add your four subscores together. Your total score should range between 24 and 120. If your score is below 24 or above 120, you have made a mistake in computing the score. Scores on each of the four communication contexts (group discussions, interpersonal conversations, meetings, and public speaking) can range from a low of 6 to a high of 30. If your score on any context is below 6 or above 30, you have made a mistake in computing the score.

The higher your score, the greater your degree of communication apprehension. The national average across the United States for the Total Score is 65.6. National averages for each of the four communication contexts are as follows: Group Discussions—15.4; Meetings—16.4; Interpersonal Conversations—14.5; Public Speaking—19.3.

TIPS FOR DEALING WITH SPEECH ANXIETY

As your textbook explains, most people are nervous when faced with the prospect of giving a speech. Your aim is not to get rid of your nerves, but to manage them so they will work for you rather than against you. Learning to do so takes practice—just as it takes practice to improve other aspects of speechmaking. You can begin by following the suggestions for dealing with nervousness explained on pages 10-15 of your textbook. In addition, try the tips listed below. Over the years, many students have found them to be extremely helpful.

1. Get to know the people in your class and find out how they feel about giving speeches. Many students report—especially at the beginning of the term—that when they arise to speak, they look up from their notes to see "all those eyes on me." Get to know "those eyes." When you do, you will find that behind them are people who are just as nervous as you are.

2. Don't worry that people in the audience will see your nervousness. In most cases, students who are certain the audience can see their shaky hands and legs are told by their classmates, "Gee, I thought you looked really calm!" Remember that you are much more aware of your nervousness than are other people. If by chance your nerves do show, you will find your classmates to be extra supportive rather than extra critical.

3. Be prepared. Some students put off working on their speeches because they are nervous about the prospect of speaking. Unfortunately, waiting until the last minute to work on a speech only increases your tension and will result in a lower grade as well. Give yourself a chance to succeed. Take time to prepare your speeches well in advance.

4. Don't get flustered by the faces of audience members as you speak. Although public speakers need to be alert to audience feedback, it's important for beginning speakers to know that, despite your best efforts, some listeners will look interested and some will not. Those who do not look interested may be tired, may be worrying about their own speech, or may just have bad listening habits. Don't let them throw you off track.

5. Visualize family members and friends in the audience. Pick out three chairs—one on each side of the room and one in the middle. Now visualize a supportive family member or friend in each chair. Be specific in your mental imaging. Visualize what they are wearing, how they are sitting, the positive expressions on their faces, the way they nod their heads in support of your ideas, etc. Practicing this visualization at home as you rehearse your speech will make it even more effective.

6. Don't worry that a single mistake will ruin your speech. Some students get quite upset whenever anything goes wrong while they are speaking. If their hands shake or their voice trembles, they think they are making a fool of themselves. Or if they forget what they are going to say for a single moment, they feel as if their whole speech is a disaster. But one mistake does not destroy an entire speech any more than missing one question on an exam means that you will fail the entire test. Remember that you will be graded on many aspects of your speech other than delivery—including topic selection, research, organization, supporting materials, audience adaptation, language use, and the like. If you stumble for a moment or two in your delivery, you can still do very well on the speech as a whole.

CHECKLIST FOR ETHICAL PUBLIC SPEAKING

		Yes	No
1.	Have I examined my goals to make sure they are ethically sound?	☐	☐
2.	Can I defend my goals for the speech if they are questioned or challenged?	☐	☐
3.	Would I want other people to know my true motives in presenting this speech?	☐	☐
4.	Have I fulfilled my ethical obligation to prepare fully for the speech?	☐	☐
5.	Have I studied and researched the speech diligently so as not to communicate erroneous or misleading information to my listeners?	☐	☐
6.	Can I vouch that the speech represents my own work, my own thinking, my own language?	☐	☐
7.	Do I cite the sources of all quotations and paraphrases?	☐	☐
8.	Is the speech free of any false or deliberately deceptive statements?	☐	☐
9.	Does the speech present statistics, testimony, and other kinds of evidence fairly and accurately?	☐	☐
10.	Does the speech contain valid reasoning?	☐	☐
11.	If the speech includes visual aids, do they present facts honestly and reliably?	☐	☐
12.	If I use emotional appeals, are they appropriate to the speech topic?	☐	☐
13.	Is the speech built upon a firm foundation of facts and logic in addition to emotional appeal?	☐	☐
14.	Do I use the power of language ethically?	☐	☐
15.	Do I avoid name-calling and other forms of abusive language?	☐	☐
16.	Does my language show respect for the right of free speech and expression?	☐	☐
17.	All in all, have I made a conscious effort to put ethical principles into practice?	☐	☐

AVOIDING PLAGIARISM

1. What is the meaning of "plagiarism"?

2. According to your textbook, what is global plagiarism? Give an example.

3. According to your textbook, what is patchwork plagiarism? Give an example.

4. According to your textbook, what is incremental plagiarism? Give an example.

5. What does it mean to paraphrase? How is paraphrasing similar to and different from quoting verbatim?

6. List three guidelines from your textbook that can help you avoid plagiarism.

LISTENING SELF-EVALUATION

How often do you indulge in the following ten bad listening habits? Check yourself carefully on each one:

HABIT	Almost always	Usually	Sometimes	Seldom	Almost never	SCORE
1. Giving in to mental distractions	___	___	___	___	___	
2. Giving in to physical distractions	___	___	___	___	___	
3. Trying to recall everything a speaker says	___	___	___	___	___	
4. Rejecting a topic as uninteresting before hearing the speaker	___	___	___	___	___	
5. Faking paying attention	___	___	___	___	___	
6. Jumping to conclusions about a speaker's meaning	___	___	___	___	___	
7. Deciding a speaker is wrong before hearing everything she or he has to say	___	___	___	___	___	
8. Judging a speaker on personal appearance	___	___	___	___	___	
9. Not paying attention to a speaker's evidence	___	___	___	___	___	
10. Focusing on delivery rather than on what the speaker says	___	___	___	___	___	

TOTAL ____

How to score:

For every "almost always" checked, give yourself a score of	2
For every "usually" checked, give yourself a score of	4
For every "sometimes" checked, give yourself a score of	6
For every "seldom" checked, give yourself a score of	8
For every "almost never" checked, give yourself a score of	10

Total score interpretation:

	Below 70	You need lots of training in listening.
	From 71–90	You listen well.
	Above 90	You listen exceptionally well.

LISTENING WORKSHEET

Practice your listening skills by completing this form as you listen to a classroom speech, a speech on videotape, or a speech outside the classroom.

1. What is the topic of the speech?

2. What is the speaker's specific purpose?

3. Which of the following methods of gaining interest and attention does the speaker use in the introduction?

   ☐ Relate the topic to the audience
   ☐ Startle the audience
   ☐ Question the audience
   ☐ Tell a story
   ☐ Invite audience participation
   ☐ Refer to a previous speaker
   ☐ State the importance of the topic
   ☐ Arouse the curiosity of the audience
   ☐ Begin with a quotation
   ☐ Refer to the occasion
   ☐ Use visual or audio aids
   ☐ Begin with humor

4. Does the speaker preview the main points of the speech in the introduction?

5. List the main points developed in the body of the speech.

6. What pattern of organization does the speaker use?

7. Are the speaker's main points clear and easy to follow? Why or why not?

8. Does the speaker use a transition or other connective between each main point of the speech?

9. Which of the following methods of reinforcing the central idea does the speaker use in the conclusion?

   ☐ Restate the main points
   ☐ Make a dramatic statement
   ☐ Challenge the audience
   ☐ End with a quotation
   ☐ Refer to the introduction
   ☐ Call for action

CLUSTERING WORKSHEET

If you are having a difficult time coming up with a speech topic, you might try brainstorming for a topic. One method of brainstorming is clustering, which is described on pages 78-80 of your textbook. Create lists of items that come to mind under each of the following nine headings. If none of the items on your lists grabs your interest, try creating sublists for those items that seem the most promising as potential topics.

People

Places

Things

_____

_____

_____

_____

_____

_____

_____

_____

_____

_____

_____

_____

_____

_____

_____

Events

Processes

Concepts

_____

_____

_____

_____

_____

_____

_____

_____

_____

_____

_____

_____

_____

_____

_____

Natural Phenomena

Problems

Plans and Policies

_____

_____

_____

_____

_____

_____

_____

_____

_____

_____

_____

_____

_____

_____

_____

SPECIFIC PURPOSE CHECKLIST

		Yes	No
1.	Is the specific purpose written as a full infinitive phrase?	❑	❑
2.	Does the specific purpose include a reference to the audience?	❑	❑
3.	Is the specific purpose phrased as a statement rather than a question?	❑	❑
4.	Is the specific purpose free of figurative language?	❑	❑
5.	Is the specific purpose limited to one distinct idea?	❑	❑
6.	Does the specific purpose indicate precisely what I plan to accomplish in the speech?	❑	❑
7.	Does the specific purpose meet the requirements of the assignment?	❑	❑
8.	Can the specific purpose be accomplished in the time allotted for the speech?	❑	❑
9.	Is the specific purpose relevant to my audience?	❑	❑
10.	Does the specific purpose deal with a non-trivial subject?	❑	❑
11.	Is the specific purpose suitable for a non-technical audience?	❑	❑

CENTRAL IDEA CHECKLIST

	Yes	No
1. Is the central idea written as a complete sentence?	☐	☐
2. Is the central idea phrased as a statement rather than a question?	☐	☐
3. Is the central idea free of figurative language?	☐	☐
4. Does the central idea clearly encapsulate the main points to be discussed in the body of the speech?	☐	☐
5. Can the central idea be adequately discussed in the time allotted for the speech?	☐	☐
6. Is the central idea relevant to the audience?	☐	☐
7. Is the central idea appropriate for a non-technical audience?	☐	☐

SPECIFIC PURPOSE AND CENTRAL IDEA EXERCISES

Below are two central ideas for speeches. For each central idea provide the general purpose, specific purpose, and main points of the speech.

General Purpose:

Specific Purpose:

Central Idea: The four stages of alcoholism are the warning stage, the danger stage, the crucial stage, and the chronic stage.

Main Points:

★

General Purpose:

Specific Purpose:

Central Idea: You should join a sorority or fraternity because of the social, academic, and economic benefits.

Main Points:

PREPARING AN AUDIENCE-ANALYSIS QUESTIONNAIRE

1. Following the example on pages 115-118 of your textbook, prepare an audience-analysis questionnaire for your next speech. Design the questionnaire carefully to elicit information about the knowledge, interest, and attitudes of your classmates with regard to your speech topic. If you are giving a persuasive speech, be sure to ask about objections listeners might have to your position.

2. Your questionnaire should have a minimum of five separate questions, with seven or eight as a maximum. By all means keep the questionnaire to a single page. Typing or printing neatly will encourage your audience to take your questions seriously. Be sure to use at least one of each of the three different types of questions discussed on pages 115-118 of your textbook: fixed-alternative questions, scale questions, and open-ended questions. The more thought you put into the questionnaire, the more likely it is to be of use to you as you prepare your speech.

3. Make enough copies of your questionnaire for each member of your class. Distribute the questionnaires on the day designated by your instructor. Make sure to put your name on the questionnaire so your classmates know to whom it should be returned.

4. After you have received the completed questionnaires, tabulate the results for each question, quantifying and converting results to percentages of the total audience whenever possible. When you can't quantify the results readily (as with open-ended questions), describe the results in a few sentences. Record results on a blank copy of the questionnaire.

5. After you have tabulated the results of your questionnaire, you should use those results to help adapt your speech to the knowledge, interests, and attitudes of your audience. This does not mean you should compromise your beliefs to get a favorable response. Nor does it mean you should use devious, unethical tactics to convince your listeners. You can remain true to yourself and to the principles of ethical speechmaking while simultaneously seeking to make your ideas as clear, appropriate, and convincing as possible.

6. Your instructor may ask you to write a brief paper based on the questionnaire. In this paper, you will need to state each of the questions in your questionnaire, explain why you included each question on the questionnaire, and summarize the results with respect to each question. You should also explain what the questionnaire revealed about the knowledge, interest, and attitudes of your audience with respect to the speech topic, what portion of the whole audience became the target audience for your speech, and what steps you took in the speech to adapt your ideas to the target audience.

AUDIENCE ANALYSIS WORKSHEET

Speaker _____ Topic _____

What is your audience for this speech?

What is the specific purpose of your speech?

In choosing your specific purpose, how will you narrow the topic so it will be appropriate to this audience?

Demographic audience analysis: What special adaptation is necessary in the speech because of the audience's

- age
- sex
- religion
- racial or ethnic background
- group membership
- other (specify)

Situational audience analysis: What special adaptation is necessary in the speech because of the audience's

- size
- response to the physical setting
- knowledge about the topic
- interest level in the topic
- attitude toward the topic
- disposition toward the speaker
- disposition toward the occasion

AUDIENCE ADAPTATION WORKSHEET

What method(s) will you use in the introduction to gain the attention and interest of your audience?

What steps will you take in the introduction to relate the topic directly to your audience?

What are the main points of the speech? Why do you plan to develop these particular main points for this audience?

Why have you selected the supporting materials you plan to use for this audience?

What steps have you taken to make your language clear and appropriate to this audience?

What adjustments will you make in delivery—rate of speech, volume, tone of voice, gestures, and the like—to communicate your ideas to this audience?

LIBRARY RESEARCH WORKSHEET

Name _____ Section _____

Topic: _____

Find three articles in the library on the subject of your next speech. The articles can be from periodicals or newspapers. Provide a complete citation for each article following the bibliographic format required by your instructor and answer the questions about each article. (See pages 32-35 of this workbook for sample bibliographic formats.)

1. Article: _____
   _____

   Did you locate this article through a periodical index?   Yes ❏   No ❏

   If you answered yes, what is the name of the index? _____

   If you answered no, how did you locate the article? _____

   Why will the article be useful for your speech? Be specific. _____
   _____
   _____

2. Article: _____
   _____

   Did you locate this article through a periodical index?   Yes ❏   No ❏

   If you answered yes, what is the name of the index? _____

   If you answered no, how did you locate the article? _____

   Why will the article be useful for your speech? Be specific. _____
   _____
   _____

3. Article: _____
   _____

   Did you locate this article through a periodical index?   Yes ❏   No ❏

   If you answered yes, what is the name of the index? _____

   If you answered no, how did you locate the article? _____

   Why will the article be useful for your speech? Be specific. _____
   _____
   _____

INTERNET RESEARCH WORKSHEET

Name _____ Section _____

Topic: _____

Find two documents from the World Wide Web on the subject of your next speech. Provide a complete citation for each document following the bibliographic format required by your instructor and answer the questions about each document. (See pages 32-35 of this workbook for sample bibliographic formats.)

1. Document: _____
   _____

   Did you locate this document through a search engine?   Yes ❑   No ❑

   If you answered yes, what is the name of the search engine? _____

   If you answered no, how did you locate the document? _____

   Why will the document be useful for your speech? Be specific. _____
   _____
   _____

   Explain why the author or sponsoring organization for this document should be accepted as a credible source on your speech topic.
   _____
   _____

2. Document: _____
   _____

   Did you locate this document through a search engine?   Yes ❑   No ❑

   If you answered yes, what is the name of the search engine? _____

   If you answered no, how did you locate the document? _____

   Why will the document be useful for your speech? Be specific. _____
   _____
   _____

   Explain why the author or sponsoring organization for this document should be accepted as a credible source on your speech topic.
   _____
   _____

SUPPORTING MATERIALS CHECKLIST

	Yes	No	Doesn't Apply
1. Do I use examples to make ideas clear to my audience?	☐	☐	☐
2. Do I use examples to personalize ideas for my audience?	☐	☐	☐
3. Do I reinforce my hypothetical examples with statistics or testimony?	☐	☐	☐
4. Are my extended examples vivid and richly textured?	☐	☐	☐
5. Have I practiced the delivery of my extended examples to give them dramatic effect?	☐	☐	☐
6. Do I use statistics to quantify my ideas?	☐	☐	☐
7. Are my statistics representative of what they purport to measure?	☐	☐	☐
8. Are my statistics from reliable sources?	☐	☐	☐
9. Do I cite the sources of my statistics?	☐	☐	☐
10. Do I use statistical measures (mean, median, mode) correctly?	☐	☐	☐
11. Do I round off complicated statistics?	☐	☐	☐
12. Do I use visual aids to clarify statistical trends?	☐	☐	☐
13. Do I explain my statistics and relate them to the audience?	☐	☐	☐
14. Do I use testimony to support my ideas?	☐	☐	☐
15. Do I use testimony from qualified sources?	☐	☐	☐
16. Do I use testimony from unbiased sources?	☐	☐	☐
17. Do I identify the sources of all testimony?	☐	☐	☐
18. Do I quote and paraphrase all sources of testimony with complete accuracy?	☐	☐	☐

SUPPORTING MATERIALS EXERCISE

Evaluate the use of supporting materials in the following speech excerpt in light of the criteria for supporting materials discussed in Chapter 7 of your textbook. Be sure to deal with all the supporting materials in each paragraph, and be specific in assessing their strengths and weaknesses.

According to emergency medicine specialist Dr. Randall Sword, emergency rooms will handle more than 160 million cases this year alone. This means that one out of every sixteen Americans will spend time in an emergency room this year. Unfortunately, the National Academy of Sciences states that "emergency medical care is one of the weakest links in the delivery of health care in the nation." In fact, medical researchers estimate that 5,000 deaths annually from poisoning, drowning, and drug overdoses, as well as 20 percent of all deaths from automobile accidents, would not have happened if the victims had received prompt and proper emergency room care.

One cause of this problem is that many doctors are not properly trained in emergency care. According to *U.S. News and World Report*, fewer than 50 percent of emergency room physicians have completed special emergency training courses. A survey by Frey and Mangold found that untrained emergency room physicians felt they were unsure how to diagnose or treat many of the extreme abdomen, chest, and cardiac disorders that often appear in hospital emergency rooms.

Another cause of the problem is that precious time is often wasted on useless paperwork before vital emergency treatment begins. Several years ago, a man driving by an elementary school in my hometown had a heart attack and crashed into a school yard. Seven children were taken to the emergency room three blocks away, but the real tragedy had not yet begun. Once in the emergency room, the children were denied treatment until their parents were contacted and the admitting forms were filled out. By the time the forms were completed, two of the children had died.

BIBLIOGRAPHY FORMATS

A bibliography should cite all the sources used in preparing a speech—including Internet documents, personal interviews, television programs, and CD-ROM publications, as well as print materials such as books, newspaper and magazine articles, reference works, government documents, and the like. There are a number of bibliographical formats, and you should check with your instructor to see which she or he wants you to follow. Examples of the two major formats—from the Modern Language Association (MLA) and the American Psychological Association (APA)—are provided below.

	Book: Single Author
MLA	Lampe, Gregory P. *Frederick Douglass: Freedom's Voice, 1818-1845*. East Lansing, MI: Michigan State UP, 1998.
APA	Lampe, G.P. (1998). *Frederick Douglass: Freedom's voice, 1818-1845*. East Lansing, MI: Michigan State University Press, 1998.
	Book: Two or More Authors
MLA	Andrews, Kevin, and Michelle Curtis. *A Changing Australia: The Social, Cultural and Economic Trends Facing Australia*. Annandale, VA: Federation Press, 1998.
APA	Andrews, K., & Curtis, M. (1998). *A changing Australia: The social, cultural and economic trends facing Australia*. Annandale, VA: Federation Press.
	Book: Second or Later Edition
MLA	Lerner, Gerda. *The Grimké Sisters from South Carolina*. 2nd ed. New York: Oxford UP, 1998.
APA	Lerner, G. (1998). *The Grimké sisters from South Carolina* (2nd ed.). New York: Oxford University Press.
	Book: Corporate Author
MLA	American Association of Cereal Chemists. *Sweeteners*. St. Paul, MN: American Association of Cereal Chemists, 1998.
APA	American Association of Cereal Chemists. (1998). *Sweeteners*. St. Paul, MN: American Association of Cereal Chemists.
	Book: Anthology or Compilation
MLA	Ram, Kalpana, and Margaret Jolly, eds. *Maternities and Modernities: Colonial and Postcolonial Experiences in Asia and the Pacific*. Cambridge: Cambridge UP, 1998.
APA	Ram, K., & Jolly, M. (Eds.). (1998). *Maternities and modernities: Colonial and postcolonial experiences in Asia and the Pacific*. Cambridge: Cambridge University Press.

Chapter in Anthology or Compilation	
MLA	Stivens, Maila. "Modernizing the Malay Mother." *Maternities and Modernities: Colonial and Postcolonial Experiences in Asia and the Pacific.* Ed. Kalpana Ram and Margaret Jolly. Cambridge: Cambridge UP, 1998. 50-80.
APA	Stivens, M. (1998). Modernizing the Malay mother. In K. Ram & M. Jolly (eds.), *Maternities and modernities: Colonial and postcolonial experiences in Asia and the Pacific* (pp. 50-80). Cambridge: Cambridge University Press.
Signed Magazine Article	
MLA	Williams, Patricia. "Speaking of Race." *Atlantic Monthly* May 1998: 9-11.
APA	Williams, P. (1998, May). Speaking of race. *Atlantic Monthly*, pp. 9-11.
Unsigned Magazine Article	
MLA	"Tracking Nuclear Weapons." *Time* 25 May 1998: 38-39.
APA	Tracking nuclear weapons. (1998, May 25). *Time*, pp. 38-39.
Journal Article, Continuous Pagination	
MLA	Smith, Grant W. "The Political Impact of Name Sounds." *Communication Monographs* 65 (1998): 154-72.
APA	Smith, G.W. (1998). The political impact of name sounds. *Communication Monographs, 65,* 154-172.
Journal Article, Noncontinuous Pagination	
MLA	Kauffman, James M., and Harold J. Burbach. "Creating Classroom Civility." *Education Digest* 63.1 (1998): 12-18.
APA	Kauffman, J.M., & Burbach, H.J. (1998). Creating Classroom Civility. *Education Digest, 63*(1), 12-18.
Signed Newspaper Article	
MLA	Price, Hugh B. "Tell Me Again: Why Are S.A.T. Scores So Crucial?" *New York Times* 26 May 1998: A23.
APA	Price, H.B. (1998, May 26). Tell me again: Why are S.A.T. scores so crucial? *New York Times*, p. A23.
Unsigned Newspaper Article	
MLA	"4.7 Million Children Qualify for Medicaid." *Los Angeles Times*, 18 May 1998: A11.
APA	4.7 million children qualify for Medicaid. (1998, May 18). *Los Angeles Times*, p. A11.

Signed Newspaper Editorial	
MLA	Emmerich, Stacy. "Equal Pay for Equal Work Still a Problem for Women." Editorial. *Wisconsin State Journal* 10 Apr.1998: A9.
APA	Emmerich, S. (1998, April 10). Equal pay for equal work still a problem for women [Editorial]. *Wisconsin State Journal*, p. A9.
Unsigned Newspaper Editorial	
MLA	"Hospitals Resist Reform, Work New Doctors Too Hard." Editorial. *USA Today* 28 May 1998: A12.
APA	Hospitals resist reform, work new doctors too hard. (1998, May 28). [Editorial]. *USA Today,* p. A12.
Government Publication	
MLA	United States. Environmental Protection Agency. *New Motor Vehicles and New Motor Vehicle Engines Air Pollution Control: Voluntary Standards for Light-Duty Vehicles.* Washington, D.C.: Government Printing Office, 1998.
APA	U.S. Environmental Protection Agency. (1998). *New motor vehicles and new motor vehicle engines air pollution control: Voluntary standards for light-duty vehicles.* Washington, D.C.: Government Printing Office.
Signed Article in Reference Work	
MLA	Chaney, Warren H. "Ventriloquism." *Collier's Encyclopedia.* New York: Collier's, 1996.
APA	Chaney, W.H. (1996). Ventriloquism. In *Collier's encyclopedia* (Vol. 23, pp. 79-80). New York: Collier's.
Unsigned Article in Reference Work	
MLA	"Morrison, Toni." *Who's Who of American Women, 1997-1998.* New Providence, NJ: Marquis Who's Who, 1996.
APA	Morrison, Toni. (1996). In *Who's who of American women, 1997-1998* (p. 766). New Providence, NJ: Marquis Who's Who.
Personal Interview	
MLA	Hernandez, Inez. Personal interview. 17 Feb. 1998.
APA	Hernandez, I. (1998, February 17). [Personal interview].
Letter or E-Mail Communication	
MLA	Ahmed, Mohammed. E-mail to the author. 5 May 1998.
APA	Ahmed, M. (mohamahmed@aol.com). (1998, May 5). *Reply to Questions for Speech.* E-mail to S. Tetrault (tetrault@sfsu.edu).

Speech or Lecture	
MLA	Chan, Yi-Huang. Lecture on water pollution. Geography 212: *Environmental Science*. University of Florida, 14 Mar.1998.
APA	Chan, Y.H. (1998, March 14). Water pollution. [Lecture]. In *Geography 212: Environmental science*. University of Florida.
Television Program	
MLA	"Crazy Like a Fox?" Narr. Ed Bradley. *60 Minutes*. CBS. WCBS, New York. 31 May 1998.
APA	Bradley, E. (Narrator). (1998, May 31). Crazy like a fox? In *60 minutes*. New York: CBS.
Film	
MLA	*Maya Lin: A Strong Clear Vision*. Dir. Freida Lee Mock. Santa Monica, CA: American Film Foundation, 1995.
APA	Mock, F.L. (Director). (1995). *Maya Lin: A strong clear vision* [Film]. Santa Monica, CA: American Film Foundation.
CD-ROM Publication	
MLA	Roundy, Robert W. "Ethiopia." *Compton's Interactive Encyclopedia*. CD-ROM. Carlsbad, CA: Compton's NewMedia, Inc., 1994.
APA	Roundy, R.W. (1994). Ethiopia. In *Compton's interactive encyclopedia* (Version 2.01). Available: [CD-ROM]. Carlsbad, CA: Compton's NewMedia, Inc.
World Wide Web Document	
MLA	Centers for Disease Control. "Preventing Foodborne Illness." 9 Aug. 1996 [last update]. <http://www.cdc.gov/ncidod/diseases/Food borne/e_coli.htm> 12 June 1998.
APA	Centers for Disease Control. (1996, August 9). Preventing foodborne illness. [Online]. Available: http://www.cdc.gov/ncidod/diseases/Food borne/e_coli.htm. [1998, 12 June].

SPEECH ORGANIZATION EXERCISE

Identify the organizational method used in each of the following sets of main points.

I. Early people did not have money but used a system of exchange based on the barter of goods and services.
II. Coin money was invented in ancient Turkey, China, and India before the birth of Christ.
III. Paper money began in China about 600 A.D. but did not become popular in the West until the 1600s.
IV. Today almost every country has an official currency tied to the international rate of exchange.

★

I. Genetic engineering is producing new plant hybrids that will vastly increase world agricultural production.
II. Genetic engineering is producing breakthroughs in medicine that will allow people to live healthier lives.
III. Genetic engineering is producing bacteria that will help clean up industrial pollutants.

★

I. Gambling addiction is an increasingly serious problem throughout the United States.
II. The problem of gambling addiction can best be solved by a combination of education and rehabilitation.

★

I. There are several causes for the destruction of the rain forests in South America.
II. If the destruction of the rain forests continues, the effects will have global impact.

★

I. The top layer of the earth is a rocky "skin" called the crust.
II. Beneath the crust is a thick layer of rock called the mantle.
III. The next lower section is a mass of melted rock called the outer core.
IV. At the center of the earth is a solid mass called the inner core.

MAIN POINTS CHECKLIST

		Yes	No
1.	Does the body of my speech contain from two to five main points?	❑	❑
2.	Are my main points organized according to one of the following methods of organization? (Check the one that applies)		
	Chronological order	❑	❑
	Spatial order	❑	❑
	Causal order	❑	❑
	Topical order	❑	❑
	Problem-solution order	❑	❑
	Problem-cause-solution order (persuasive speeches only)	❑	❑
	Comparative advantages order (persuasive speeches only)	❑	❑
	Monroe's motivated sequence (persuasive speeches only)	❑	❑
3.	Are my main points clearly separate from one another?	❑	❑
4.	As much as possible, have I used the same pattern of wording for all my main points?	❑	❑
5.	Have I roughly balanced the amount of time devoted to each main point?	❑	❑
6.	Is each main point backed up with strong, credible supporting materials?	❑	❑
7.	Do I use connectives to make sure my audience knows when I am moving from one main point to another?	❑	❑

CONNECTIVES EXERCISE

As discussed on pages 211-215 of your textbook, connectives are words or phrases that connect the ideas of a speech and indicate the relationships among them. Below are excerpts from two speech outlines—one on immigration, the other on the shortage of nurses in U.S. hospitals. For each outline, provide the connective(s) indicated in the space provided.

I. Over the years, millions of people have immigrated to the United States.
   A. Since the American Revolution, an estimated 60 million people have immigrated to the U.S.
   B. Today there are over 20 million Americans who were born in other countries.

Transition: _____
_____
_____

II. There are several reasons why people immigrate to the United States.
    A. Many people immigrate in search of economic opportunity.
    B. Others immigrate to attain political freedom.
    C. Still others immigrate to escape religious persecution.

Internal Summary: _____
_____
_____
_____

★

I. The shortage of nurses has become a serious national problem.
   A. More than 60 percent of U.S. hospitals have nurse shortages severe enough to threaten the quality of health care.
   B. Experts warn that the shortage will become even worse in the years ahead unless steps are taken to solve it.

Transition and Internal Preview: _____
_____
_____
_____

II. The problem can be solved by offering nurses better salaries and better working conditions.
    A. Better salaries will attract more people to nursing as a profession.
    B. Better working conditions will improve morale and reduce burnout among nurses.

SPEECH INTRODUCTION CHECKLIST

	Yes	No
1. Do I gain the attention and interest of my audience by (check all that apply):		
Relating the speech topic to my audience	☐	☐
Stating the importance of my topic	☐	☐
Startling the audience	☐	☐
Arousing the curiosity of the audience	☐	☐
Questioning the audience	☐	☐
Beginning with a quotation	☐	☐
Telling a story	☐	☐
Referring to the occasion	☐	☐
Inviting audience participation	☐	☐
Using audio equipment or visual aids	☐	☐
Relating to a previous speaker	☐	☐
Beginning with humor	☐	☐
2. Do I clearly reveal the topic of my speech?	☐	☐
3. Do I establish my credibility to speak on this topic?	☐	☐
4. If my topic is controversial, do I take steps to establish my goodwill toward the audience?	☐	☐
5. Do I provide a preview statement of the main points to be covered in the body of the speech?	☐	☐
6. Do I define any key terms that will be necessary for the audience to understand the rest of my speech?	☐	☐
7. Do I have a transition between the introduction and the body of my speech?	☐	☐
8. Is the introduction limited to 10-20 percent of my entire speech?	☐	☐
9. Have I worked out the language of my introduction in detail?	☐	☐
10. Have I practiced the delivery of my introduction so I can present it fluently, confidently, and with strong eye contact?	☐	☐
11. Have I visualized myself approaching the lectern confidently, establishing eye contact with my audience, and starting the speech without rushing?	☐	☐

SPEECH CONCLUSION CHECKLIST

	Yes	No
1. Do I signal that my speech is coming to an end?	☐	☐
2. Do I reinforce my central idea by (check all that apply):		
Summarizing the main points of my speech	☐	☐
Ending with a quotation	☐	☐
Making a dramatic statement	☐	☐
Referring to the introduction	☐	☐
3. Is the conclusion limited to 5-10 percent of my entire speech?	☐	☐
4. Have I worked out the language of my conclusion in detail?	☐	☐
5. Have I practiced the delivery of my conclusion so I can present it fluently, confidently, and with strong eye contact?	☐	☐
6. Have I visualized myself maintaining eye contact with my audience and waiting confidently for applause after concluding rather than rushing to my seat?	☐	☐

ASSESSING SPEECH INTRODUCTIONS

Below are four complete introductions from classroom speeches. Each has at least one flaw that keeps it from fulfilling all the major functions of an effective introduction discussed on pages 222-235 of your textbook: (1) Gain the attention and interest of the audience; (2) Reveal the topic of the speech; (3) Establish credibility and goodwill; (4) Preview the body of the speech. In each case identify the flaw (or flaws) and make specific suggestions for improving the introduction.

1. What tiny crystal fortified the coffers of many ancient empires and laid waste to others? What mineral has the power to create and the power to destroy? What is "good as gold" when scarce and "cheap as dirt" when abundant?

   The answer to all of these questions is salt, the spice of life. Today I would like to look at the importance of salt in history, at how we spice up our lives with salt today, and at the role salt will probably play in the future.

2. We have so much unused human potential. By improving the use of your time, you can have much more time for social activities. You can use your mental processes more fully, thereby improving your grades. You can also increase your physical stamina and improve your health. We must learn to know our bodies.

3. A six-year-old collie lay battered and helpless by the side of the road. The car that hit her had broken her pelvis, dislocated her hip, and smashed her jaw. It had also blinded her, and she whimpered in pain and fear.

   Unfortunately, this true story happens much too frequently because of the growing problem of pet overpopulation. Having grown up on a farm with animals of all kinds, I care deeply about their welfare, and I have become aware through my veterinary courses of how serious the problem of pet overpopulation is.

4. Every problem has at least two sides. When one side is right, and the other side is wrong, the problem is easy to solve. But what if both sides have merit in their arguments? How do you solve these problems?

   Balancing the rights of everyone in an adoption is one of these problems. The parents who give up the child have a right that all the information they disclose be kept confidential, while the adopted child has a right to know about the identity of his or her natural parents.

   Today I'd like to explore this problem with you and look at one approach to solving it.

PREPARATION OUTLINE GUIDE

The following is a guide to use as you develop preparation outlines for your speeches. For purposes of illustration, this guide has three main points in the body of the speech. In your speeches, the number and organization of main points, subpoints, and sub-subpoints will vary depending on the topic and purpose of any given speech. However, the elements needed in the outline—title, specific purpose statement, central idea, introduction, body, conclusion, connectives, bibliography—will remain the same. For more information, check the guidelines for preparation outlines and the sample preparation outline with commentary on pages 246-253 of your textbook.

Name:
Date:
Section:

TITLE

[Check with your instructor to see if you need to include a title with your outline. If you do, be sure to consult the discussion of speech titles on pages 250-251 of your textbook.]

Specific Purpose Statement: [Should fit the criteria for specific purpose statements on pages 84-89 of your textbook.]

Central Idea: [Should fit the criteria for central ideas on pages 89-94 of your textbook.]

INTRODUCTION

[Check with your instructor to see whether the introduction should be written out word for word or presented in outline form. In either case, label the introduction as a distinct section of the speech and make sure it fulfills all four major objectives of an introduction explained on pages 222-235 of your textbook: (1) Gain the attention and interest of the audience; (2) Reveal the topic of the speech; (3) Establish credibility and goodwill; (4) Preview the body of the speech.]

(*Connective:* Make sure the audience knows you are moving from the introduction into the first main point of the body. For information on connectives, review pages 211-215 of your textbook.)

BODY

I. A single complete sentence expressing the main point of this section of the speech.
    A. Subpoint [As with main points, subpoints should be written in full sentences.]
        1. Sub-subpoint [Check with your instructor to see whether sub-subpoints need to be written as full sentences.]
        2. Sub-subpoint
    B. Subpoint

(*Connective*: Use a transition or other connective to help the audience move with you from one main point to the next.)

II.   A single complete sentence expressing the main point of this section of the speech.
    A. Subpoint
    B. Subpoint
        1. Sub-subpoint
            a. Sub-sub-subpoint
            b. Sub-sub-subpoint
        2. Sub-subpoint

(*Connective*: Use a transition or other connective to help the audience move with you from one main point to the next.)

III. A single complete sentence expressing the main point of this section of the speech.
    A. Subpoint
        1. Sub-subpoint
        2. Sub-subpoint
    B. Subpoint
        1. Sub-subpoint
        2. Sub-subpoint
        3. Sub-subpoint
    C. Subpoint

(*Connective*: Use a transition or other connective to help the audience move with you from the body of your speech to the conclusion.)

CONCLUSION

[Check with your instructor to see whether the conclusion should be written out word for word or presented in outline form. In either case, label the conclusion as a distinct section of the speech and make sure it fulfills both major objectives of a conclusion explained on pages 235-240 of your textbook: (1) Let the audience know you are ending the speech; (2) Reinforce the audience's understanding of, or commitment to, the central idea.]

BIBLIOGRAPHY

[Here you list complete citations for the research materials used in preparing your speech. The two major bibliographic formats are those recommended by the Modern Language Association (MLA) and the American Psychological Association (APA). Sample citations for both are provided on pages 32-35 of this workbook. Check with your instructor to see which format you should use for your bibliography.]

PREPARATION OUTLINE CHECKLIST

		Yes	No
1.	Does my speech have a title, if one is required?	☐	☐
2.	Do I state the specific purpose before the text of the outline itself?	☐	☐
3.	Do I state the central idea before the text of the outline itself?	☐	☐
4.	Are the introduction, body, and conclusion clearly labeled?	☐	☐
5.	Are main points and subpoints written in full sentences?	☐	☐
6.	Are transitions, internal summaries, and internal previews clearly labeled?	☐	☐
7.	Does the outline follow a consistent pattern of symbolization and indentation?	☐	☐
8.	Does the outline provide a clear visual framework that shows the relationships among the ideas of my speech?	☐	☐
9.	Does the bibliography identify all the sources I consulted in preparing the speech?	☐	☐
10.	Does the bibliography follow the format required by my instructor?	☐	☐

SCRAMBLED OUTLINE EXERCISE

In the left-hand column below is a blank outline from a speech about parachuting. In the right-hand column, arranged in random order, are the subpoints and sub-subpoints to fill in the outline. Choose the appropriate subpoint or sub-subpoint for each blank in the outline.

Outline

I. The history of parachuting goes back 1,000 years.

   A.

   B.

   C.

   D.

   E.

II. The two major types of parachutes employed today are the traditional military style and the more modern parafoil.

   A.

      1.

      2.

         a.

         b.

   B.

      1.

      2.

      3.

Subpoints and Sub-Subpoints

Their rate of descent is 18-22 feet per second.

The first successful parachute jump was in 1797 by Frenchman Andre-Jacques Garnerin.

Even with the necessary training, 5 percent of military parachutists will be injured on impact during any given jump.

Their slow rate of descent and ability to "brake" make parafoils ideal for skydivers and other civilian parachutists.

In the twentieth century parachuting has been used mainly for fire fighting, troop deployment, and recreation.

Landing safely at this force requires a great deal of training.

Parafoils are markedly slower and safer than military parachutes.

At this rate of descent a miliary parachutist lands with a force equivalent to jumping off a one-story building.

In 1147 a Turk leaped to his death trying to parachute off a tall building.

Military parachutes are designed to descend quickly.

In addition to descending more slowly than military parachutes, parafoils can be "braked" before impact.

By 1830 parachutists were jumping in front of large crowds as a form of entertainment.

They descend at a rate of 12-15 feet per second.

In 1485 Leonardo Da Vinci sketched a parachute design that modern engineers say would have worked.

QUESTION-AND-ANSWER SESSIONS

1. If your speech is followed by a question-and-answer session, you need to take that session as seriously as the speech itself. Because the question-and-answer session is the last thing the audience hears, it can leave a strong lasting impression. The impact of even a well-prepared speech can be undermined by a speaker who is unable to answer questions effectively. On the other hand, a speaker who answers questions adeptly can strengthen the impact of the speech and, in the process, substantially enhance his or her credibility.

2. Anticipate possible questions and formulate answers in advance. If you are giving a persuasive speech, be sure you are ready to answer possible objections that the audience may have to your position.

3. Repeat or paraphrase each question after it is asked. This is especially important when speaking to a large audience that may not be able to hear the question clearly. Repeating the question also gives you a moment to frame your answer before you respond.

4. When confronted with an unclear or unwieldy question, try to rephrase it by saying something like, "If I understand your question, it seems to me that you are asking . . ."

5. When you are being asked a question, look at the questioner. Direct your answer, however, to the entire audience. Make occasional eye contact with the questioner as you answer, but speak primarily to the audience as a whole.

6. Allow one follow-up question from each questioner, but do not allow yourself to be dragged into a personal debate with any questioner.

7. Answer questions clearly, briefly, and directly. Don't be afraid to admit that you don't know the answer to a factual question. Ask whether someone in the audience knows the answer. If no one responds, tell the questioner you will check into the answer as soon as possible after the speech.

8. Avoid responding defensively even to hostile questions. Regard the question-and-answer session as another opportunity to communicate your ideas, rather than as a challenge to your competence, intelligence, or personhood. If someone in the audience has misunderstood a portion of your speech, the question-and-answer session is an excellent opportunity to clarify your ideas.

9. Don't let one person dominate the question-and-answer session. If someone launches into an extended monologue instead of asking a question, or keeps asking one question after another, respond by saying something like, "Those are very interesting ideas, but we need to give other people a chance to ask questions as well. Why don't we talk individually after the speech?"

10. Make sure the question-and-answer session does not run too long. In most situations, there will be a predetermined length of time for the question-and-answer session or for the speech and question-and-answer session combined. When that time arrives, respond to the last question and thank the audience for its time and attention.

TIPS FOR THE SPEAKING OUTLINE

1. Keep your speaking outline as brief as possible. Reduce your speech to key words and phrases (except for direct quotations, statistics, source citations, and certain key ideas) to enhance the extemporaneous quality of your delivery.

2. Follow the visual framework of symbolization and indentation used in your preparation outline. This will make it easier for you to see where you are in the speech at any given moment.

3. Some people put their speaking outlines on index cards; others prefer to write them on paper or to print them from a word processor. Either can work fine as long as your notes are immediately legible to you while you are speaking. Check with your instructor to see if she or he has any preferences in this regard.

4. Most speakers who use index cards find the 3 X 5 size too cramped and prefer the 4 X 6 or 5 X 8 sizes instead.

5. If you put your speaking outline on index cards, try to use one card for each main point, plus one card each for the introduction and conclusion. This will reinforce the distinctiveness of each point and will help you pause at appropriate moments during the speech.

6. Whether you use index cards or regular paper, write on only one side of each card or sheet of paper. Limit the amount of information on each card or sheet of paper so you can read it at a glance under the pressure of the speech situation. Number each card or sheet of paper in the upper right-hand corner so it is easy for you to make sure they are in the correct order.

7. If you compose your speaking outline on a word processor, use a large, readable font. It is not a good idea to use all capital letters, since research has shown that a lot of words in ALL CAPS is harder to read than is normal text. Use generous margins and provide extra space between lines.

8. If you are composing your outline on a word processor and want to use index cards for your speaking notes, format the pages on your word processor to correspond with the size of your index cards. You can then print your notes on computer paper and tape or glue them to your index cards.

9. If you write your speaking outline by hand, do not use pencil, which smudges easily and is often too light to read without straining.

10. Give yourself cues for delivering the speech. Remind yourself to maintain eye contact and to gesture. Tell yourself when to pause, where to speak louder, and the like. Also include signals that will remind you when to display and remove visual aids. Use highlighters or brightly colored markers for delivery cues to make sure you will not overlook them during the speech.

11. Prepare your speaking outline far enough in advance that you will have plenty of time to practice with it as you rehearse the speech.

TIPS FOR SPEAKING FROM A MANUSCRIPT

1. Write your speech for the ear. It should be prepared with simple words, short sentences, and the rhythm of conversation. As you work on the speech, keep saying the lines out loud, listening for the rhythms of oral style. If possible, use a tape recorder to record your first draft. Listen to yourself to find the awkward phrases that need revision.

2. Make sure your manuscript is easy to read. Use wide margins and double or triple space between lines. Use a large font that can be deciphered at a glance. Do not use all capital letters, since research has shown that they are harder to read than a combination of capital letters and lower-case letters. Print the manuscript on bond paper that will not crinkle or roll up at the edges.

3. Do not recite the manuscript word for word when you deliver the speech. Instead, look down at the page, "photograph" a phrase in your mind, and deliver the phrase. Try not to speak when your eyes are fixed on the page. Talk through the text, rather than worrying about saying every word just as it is written. You are the only person who will know when the speech departs slightly from the manuscript.

4. Don't try to "photograph" too much text at a time. Let your eye record what you can remember comfortably, then look up and speak to the audience. Break sentences into oral chunks. Strive for bite-sized groups of words that are comfortable to utter in one breath.

5. Don't be afraid to pause between statements. At first, this may feel awkward, but frequent pauses are a normal part of everyday conversation and they will not seem unnatural to your audience.

6. Establish eye contact with your audience while you are speaking. Look for someone who seems to be listening intently and speak to that person. Then switch your attention to another part of the room and engage someone else's gaze. The quickest way to lose your audience is to spend the entire speech staring at your manuscript in an effort to recite every word just the way it is written.

7. Use vocal variety to give your speech impact. Your words must be given time to sink in and to register with the audience. Remember that your listeners cannot see your speech—they can only hear it.

8. Mark your speaking text to indicate places where you want to speed up, slow down, speak louder or softer, pause, and the like. There is a key word in every line. Find that word, underline it on your text, and be sure to give it proper emphasis when you speak.

9. Practice. Delivering a speech effectively from manuscript takes time and effort. In many ways, it is harder than speaking extemporaneously. The more your practice, the more likely you are to present the speech with strong eye contact and a conversational tone.

OUT-OF-CLASS SPEECH OBSERVATION: DELIVERY

Your name _____ Speaker _____

Where was the speech presented? _____

What was the occasion for the speech? _____

Vocal Communication: *Record your observations about each of the following aspects of the speaker's voice.*

Volume _____

Pitch _____

Rate _____

Pauses _____

Vocal variety _____

Pronunciation _____

Articulation _____

Nonverbal Communication: *Record your observations about each of the following aspects of the speaker's nonverbal communication.*

Personal appearance _____

Bodily action _____

Gestures _____

Eye contact _____

Overall Evaluation of Delivery: *Explain how the speaker's delivery added to or detracted from the message.*

_____

_____

_____

What It Means For Me: *Explain at least two techniques of delivery used by the speaker that you might want to try in your next speech.*

_____

_____

CHECKLIST FOR PREPARING VISUAL AIDS

		Yes	No	Doesn't Apply
1.	Have I prepared my visual aids well in advance?	❑	❑	❑
2.	Are my visual aids clear and easy to comprehend?	❑	❑	❑
3.	Does each visual aid contain only the information that is needed to make my point?	❑	❑	❑
4.	Are my visual aids large enough to be seen clearly by everyone in the room?	❑	❑	❑
5.	Do the colors on my visual aids work well together?	❑	❑	❑
6.	Is there a clear contrast between the lettering and background on my charts, graphs, and drawings?	❑	❑	❑
7.	Do I use line graphs, pie graphs, and bar graphs correctly to show statistical trends and patterns?	❑	❑	❑
8.	Do I limit charts to no more than eight items?	❑	❑	❑
9.	Do my computer-generated aids use fonts that are easy to read?	❑	❑	❑
10.	Do my computer-generated aids contain a limited number of fonts?	❑	❑	❑
11.	Have I enlarged my photographs or converted them to overhead transparencies so they can be seen without being passed among the audience?	❑	❑	❑
12.	Are my videotapes carefully edited and incorporated into the speech?	❑	❑	❑
13.	Have I prepared my overhead transparencies in advance?	❑	❑	❑
14.	Is the print on my overhead transparencies at least one-quarter inch high?	❑	❑	❑
15.	Have I carefully planned the content, order, and timing of my multimedia presentation so it will be smooth and professional?	❑	❑	❑
16.	Do I have a backup disk for my multimedia presentation?	❑	❑	❑
17.	Am I prepared to give my speech even if the multimedia equipment were to fail?	❑	❑	❑

CHECKLIST FOR PRESENTING VISUAL AIDS

	Yes	No	Doesn't Apply
1. Can I present my visual aids without writing or drawing on the chalkboard?	☐	☐	☐
2. Have I checked the speech room to decide where I can display my visual aids most effectively?	☐	☐	☐
3. Is my posterboard sturdy enough to be displayed without curling up or falling over?	☐	☐	☐
4. Have I practiced presenting my visual aids so they will be clearly visible to everyone in the audience?	☐	☐	☐
5. Have I practiced setting up and taking down my visual aids so I can do both smoothly during the speech?	☐	☐	☐
6. Have I practiced keeping eye contact with my audience while presenting my visual aids?	☐	☐	☐
7. Have I practiced explaining my visual aids clearly and concisely in terms my audience will understand?	☐	☐	☐
8. Have I planned to distribute handouts after the speech rather than during it?	☐	☐	☐
9. Have I double checked all equipment—overhead projector, VCR, computer, etc.—to make sure it works properly?	☐	☐	☐
10. Have I rehearsed my speech with all the equipment I will use during the final presentation?	☐	☐	☐

INFORMATIVE SPEECH TOPICS

As your textbook explains, there are limitless possibilities for speech topics—including topics you already know a lot about, topics you want to learn more about, and topics you discover through one or another brainstorming procedure. If you are having trouble coming up with a topic for your informative speech, check pages 76-82 of the textbook for advice. The topics listed below are meant to provide an additional spur to your creativity as you think about a subject for your speech.

advertising	flamenco dancing	oriental rugs
aerobics	fly fishing	parenting
African literature	Geronimo	peppers
Amelia Earhardt	ginseng	pets
animal behavior	glass	photography
antique furniture	graffiti	physical therapy
artificial intelligence	guitars	Picasso
asteroids	gymnastics	plastic surgery
asthma	headaches	pyramids
Aztecs	homeopathy	Quakers
bagpipes	horse racing	quicksand
ballet	human genome project	robots
batik	hurricanes	rock climbing
bats	interior design	rodeos
bicycles	Internet	ROTC
birth order	inventions	Russian culture
braiding	Ireland	sharks
Buddhism	Japanese tea ceremony	sleep deprivation
cartography	jazz	Spain
Chinese New Year	job interviews	spiders
chiropractic	Judaism	stock market
civil rights movement	kayaking	stress
Cleopatra	Koran	study abroad
computers	Kwanzaa	sushi
cooking	landscape architecture	table tennis
Costa Rica	laughter	tattoos
cryogenics	lizards	television news
dams	Malcolm X	Thailand
Dead Sea scrolls	martial arts	tobacco
diamonds	military service	Trail of Tears
diets	motorcycles	urban planning
dream catchers	mushrooms	vegetarianism
druids	mythology	Venice
earthquakes	music therapy	volcanoes
Ellis Island	national parks	water
engineering	New Zealand	women's health
extraterrestrial intelligence	nursing	xerography
fencing	nutrition	Yosemite
fertility drugs	opera	youth sports
fire prevention	Olympic Games	zoos

INFORMATIVE SPEECH PREPARATION WORKSHEET

Name _____ Section _____

1. What is the topic of your speech? Why is it appropriate for you? _____
   _____
   _____
   _____

2. Why is the topic appropriate for your audience? _____
   _____
   _____
   _____

3. How is your topic narrowed to conform to the time limits for the speech assignment?
   _____
   _____
   _____

4. What is your specific purpose statement? _____
   _____
   _____

5. Can you answer yes to all the questions on the Specific Purpose Checklist on page 22 of this workbook? _____

6. What is your central idea? _____
   _____
   _____

7. Can you answer yes to all the questions on the Central Idea Checklist on page 23 of this workbook? _____

8. What method(s) of gaining attention do you use in the introduction? _____
   _____
   _____

9. How do you establish your credibility in the introduction? _____
   _____
   _____

—over—

54 *The Art of Public Speaking Workbook*

10. Write the preview statement you will use in your introduction. _____
_____
_____
_____

11. Can you answer yes to all the questions on the Speech Introduction Checklist on page 39 of this workbook? _____

12. What method of organization do you use in the speech? _____

13. State in full sentences the main points to be developed in the body of your speech.
_____
_____
_____
_____
_____
_____

14. Can you answer yes to all the questions on the Main Points Checklist on page 37 of this workbook? _____

15. What steps have you taken to adapt the content of your speech so it will be clear and interesting to your audience? Be specific.
_____
_____
_____
_____
_____
_____

16. What method(s) of reinforcing your central idea do you use in the conclusion?
_____
_____

17. Can you answer yes to all the questions on the Speech Conclusion Checklist on page 40 of this workbook? _____

INFORMATIVE SPEECH SELF-ASSESSMENT

Your task is to review your informative speech and to reach a full, objective assessment of its major strengths and weaknesses. Write a thoughtful evaluation of the speech in full-sentence and paragraph form with an introduction and a conclusion.

Be specific and concrete in your comments. Note in particular the areas in which you believe you did especially well and those areas in which you want to make special improvement in the next speech. Explain why you had difficulty with certain aspects of this speech and indicate the specific steps you will take to improve your next presentation.

Use the following questions to guide your self-assessment, though you do not need to answer each question individually in your paper. Be specific and concrete in your comments.

Topic and Purpose
    Was the topic appropriate for the audience and the occasion?
    Did you have a clear specific purpose that you could accomplish in the allotted time?

Organization
    Was the speech well organized?
    Did you fulfill all the major functions of a speech introduction?
    Did you fulfill all the major objectives of a speech conclusion?
    Were the main points of the body clear and easy to follow?
    Did you use connectives effectively?

Supporting Materials, Audience Adaptation, and Language
    Did you conduct adequate research when preparing the speech?
    Did you adapt your speech so it would be relevant and interesting to your audience?
    Did you follow the criteria in your textbook for the effective use of supporting materials?
    Did you make a conscious effort to use clear, nontechnical language?

Delivery and Visual Aids
    Did you begin and end your speech without rushing?
    Did you use pauses, rate, pitch, and vocal variety effectively in delivering the speech?
    Did your nonverbal communication add to or detract from the speech?
    Did you maintain strong eye contact throughout the speech?
    If you used visual aids, were they carefully prepared and smoothly integrated into the speech?
    Did you follow the guidelines in your textbook for presenting visual aids?

Overall Assessment
    What were you most pleased with in the speech? What were you least pleased with?
    If you had an opportunity to deliver this speech again next week, what changes would you make? Be specific.

PERSUASIVE SPEECH TOPICS

As your textbook explains, there are limitless possibilities for speech topics—including topics you already know a lot about, topics you want to learn more about, and topics that you discover through one or another brainstorming procedure. If you are having trouble coming up with a topic for your persuasive speech, check pages 76-82 of the textbook for advice. The topics listed below are meant to provide an additional spur to your creativity as you think about a subject for your speech.

adoption laws
advertising in schools
affirmative action
age discrimination
agriculture
AIDS
airbags
airplane safety
alcohol abuse
alternate energy sources
animal testing
boat safety
breast cancer
campaign finance reform
campus safety
censorship
chewing tobacco
child abuse
child labor
child-custody laws
church-state separation
cloning
coastal erosion
college athletics
college tuition
community service
consumer rights
court system
crime prevention
death penalty
decaying bridges
diplomatic immunity
disability laws
DNA fingerprinting
doctor-assisted suicide
domestic terrorism
drug laws
drunk driving
education reform
electoral college

emergency rooms
endangered species
English-only laws
environmental pollution
flat tax
food safety
foreign aid
funding for the arts
gambling
gay rights
genetic engineering
Gulf War syndrome
gun control
health laboratories
home schooling
homelessness
human rights
hunger
illiteracy
identity theft
immigration laws
international terrorism
Internet security
insanity defense
juvenile murderers
labor laws
logging
magnet schools
mail-order fraud
managed care
mass transportation
medical malpractice
mining
minimum wage
motorcycle helmet laws
music ratings
national defense
national health system
national parks
noise pollution

nuclear testing
nurse shortage
organ donation
personal health
prison system
privacy laws
pesticides
political corruption
poverty
pornography
prayer in schools
prostitution
public transportation
responsible journalism
road rage
school-bus safety
school choice
sex education
sexual harassment
sickle-cell anemia
smokeless tobacco
Social Security
space exploration
speech codes
speed limits
standardized tests
student loans
sweat shops
telephone deregulation
television violence
tenants' rights
truth in adverting
tuberculosis
vandalism
victims' rights
volunteering
voting in elections
water purity
water rights
women in the military

FACT, VALUE, OR POLICY?

As explained on pages 375-385 of your textbook, persuasive speeches can be given on questions of fact, questions of value, or questions of policy. Below are four specific purpose statements for persuasive speeches. In each case explain whether the speech associated with it concerns a question of fact, value, or policy. Then rewrite the specific purpose statement to make it appropriate for a speech about one of the other two kinds of questions. For instance, if the original purpose statement is about a question of policy, write a new specific purpose statement that deals with the same topic as either a question of fact or a question of value.

1. To persuade my audience to get training in CPR.

   A. Does this specific purpose deal with a question of fact, value, or policy? _____

   B. Rewritten specific purpose statement: _____
   _____
   _____

2. To persuade my audience that pornography is a major cause of violence against women.

   A. Does this specific purpose deal with a question of fact, value, or policy? _____

   B. Rewritten specific purpose statement: _____
   _____
   _____

3. To persuade my audience that a national ban on private ownership of all kinds of guns should be adopted to help decrease violence.

   A. Does this specific purpose deal with a question of fact, value, or policy? _____

   B. Rewritten specific purpose statement: _____
   _____
   _____

4. To persuade my audience that it is unethical for U.S. clothing companies to employ foreign workers at substandard wages.

   A. Does this specific purpose deal with a question of fact, value, or policy? _____

   B. Rewritten specific purpose statement: _____
   _____
   _____

EVIDENCE CHECKLIST

		Yes	No
1.	Are all of my claims supported by evidence?	❑	❑
2.	Do I use sufficient evidence to convince my audience of my claims?	❑	❑
3.	Is my evidence stated in specific rather than general terms?	❑	❑
4.	Do I use evidence that is new to my audience?	❑	❑
5.	Is my evidence from credible, unbiased sources?	❑	❑
6.	Do I identify the sources of my evidence?	❑	❑
7.	Is my evidence clearly linked to each point that it is meant to prove?	❑	❑
8.	Do I provide evidence to answer possible objections the audience may have to my position?	❑	❑
9.	Does my evidence include a mix of the three major kinds of supporting materials—statistics, examples, and testimony?	❑	❑
10.	Can I answer yes to all the questions on the Supporting Materials Checklist on page 30 of this workbook?	❑	❑

PERSUASIVE SPEECH PREPARATION WORKSHEET

Name _____ Section _____

1. What is the topic of your speech? _____

2. Are you speaking on a question of fact, value, or policy? _____

3. What is your specific purpose statement? _____
   _____
   _____

4. Can you answer yes to all the questions on the Specific Purpose Checklist on page 22 of this workbook? _____

5. Is your speech meant to achieve passive agreement or immediate action from your audience?
   _____

6. What is your central idea? _____
   _____
   _____

7. Can you answer yes to all the questions on the Central Idea Checklist on page 23 of this workbook? _____

8. What is the target audience for your speech? How will you adapt your speech to be persuasive to your target audience? Be specific.
   _____
   _____
   _____
   _____

9. What method(s) of gaining attention do you use in the introduction? _____
   _____
   _____

10. How do you establish your credibility in the introduction? _____
    _____
    _____
    _____

—over—

11. Write the preview statement you will use in your introduction. _____
_____
_____
_____

12. Can you answer yes to all the questions on the Speech Introduction Checklist on page 39 of this workbook? _____

13. What method of organization do you use in the speech? _____

14. State in full sentences the main points to be developed in the body of your speech.
_____
_____
_____
_____
_____

15. Can you answer yes to all the questions on the Main Points Checklist on page 37 of this workbook? _____

16. What supporting materials do you use in developing each main point? Be specific.
_____
_____
_____
_____
_____

17. Can you answer yes to all the questions on the Evidence Checklist on page 58 of this workbook? _____

18. What steps have you taken to answer potential objections that your audience may have to your position? Be specific.
_____
_____
_____
_____

19. What method(s) of reinforcing your central idea do you use in the conclusion?
_____
_____

20. Can you answer yes to all the questions on the Speech Conclusion Checklist on page 40 of this workbook? _____

REASONING EXERCISE

Below are eight statements, each of which illustrates one of the fallacies in reasoning discussed on pages 413-424 of your textbook: hasty generalization, false cause, invalid analogy, red herring, *ad hominem*, either-or, bandwagon, and slippery slope. Identify the fallacy in each statement and explain why the statement is fallacious.

1. I don't see any reason to wear a helmet when I ride a bike. Everyone bikes without a helmet.

2. It's ridiculous to worry about protecting America's national parks against pollution and overuse when innocent people are being killed by domestic terrorists.

3. There can be no doubt that the Great Depression was caused by Herbert Hoover. He became President in March 1929, and the stock market crashed just seven months later.

4. If we allow the school board to spend money remodeling the gymnasium, next they will want to build a new school and give all the teachers a huge raise. Taxes will soar so high that businesses will leave and then there will be no jobs for anyone in this town.

5. Raising a child is just like having a pet—you need to feed it, play with it, and everything will be fine.

6. I can't support Representative Frey's proposal for campaign finance reform. After all, he was kicked out of law school for cheating on an exam.

7. One nonsmoker, interviewed at a restaurant, said, "I can eat dinner just fine even though people around me are smoking." Another, responding to a *Los Angeles Times* survey, said, "I don't see what all the fuss is about. My wife has smoked for years and it has never bothered me." We can see, then, that secondhand smoke does not cause a problem for most nonsmokers.

8. Our school must either increase tuition or cut back on library services for students.

SPEECH OUTLINE IN MONROE'S MOTIVATED SEQUENCE

A FRIEND IN NEED
Sandy Hefty

Specific Purpose: To persuade my audience to volunteer time to help needy elderly people remain in their homes.

Central Idea: By participating in a volunteer program, college students can help needy elderly people continue to live independently in their homes.

Introduction

[Attention]
I. Story of Loretta Olson, an 85-year-old woman who suffers from Alzheimer's disease.
II. During my freshman year, I volunteered six hours a week to help Loretta remain independent in her home.
III. Like Loretta, there are millions of elderly Americans who need help to remain independent in their homes.
IV. In my class survey, all but two of you said you have living grandparents, and seven of you said you have grandparents who live alone.
V. Today I would like to persuade you to help solve the problems facing less fortunate elderly Americans by volunteering time to help them remain independent in their homes.

(Transition: Let's begin by addressing the problems that can occur among this group of people.)

Body

[Need]
I. There are two problems that can occur when elderly people living alone do not get the companionship and care they need.
  A. The first problem is that elderly people may not be able to meet all of their physical needs.
   1. Example of an 87-year-old woman whom I helped as a volunteer.
   2. Like this woman, many elderly people can live alone but need help with cleaning, food preparation, and transportation.
  B. The second problem is suicide.
   1. According to the National Center for Vital Statistics, people age 75 and older have the highest rate of suicide compared to all other groups.
   2. That high suicide rate stems from three major causes: helplessness, hopelessness, and haplessness.
    a. Helplessness describes the feelings of powerlessness some elderly people feel upon realizing they're losing their physical and mental vigor.
    b. Hopelessness is associated with depression caused by the realization of the onset of old age.
    c. Haplessness refers to a series of repeated losses, such as loss of earnings, friends, and family.

(Transition: Now that we have talked about the two major problems facing elderly people who do not get the companionship and care they need, let's talk about what we can do to help solve these problems.)

[Satisfaction] II. As individuals, we can help solve these problems by getting involved with a volunteer program that assists elderly people who need help living at home.
A. Here in Wisconsin, the Community Options Program is designed to help the elderly and people with disabilities stay out of nursing homes.
B. Right here in Madison, the Independent Living program provides companionship and assistance for elderly people who live at home.

[Visualization] III. It is practical and rewarding for college students to get involved with such programs.
A. You decide how much time to volunteer based on your individual schedule.
1. You can volunteer for as few as one or two hours a week.
2. You can volunteer for as many as forty hours a week.
B. You will experience great personal gratification by helping people less fortunate than yourself.
C. You can even receive financial assistance for participating in some volunteer programs.
1. Both the state-run Community Options Program and the federally-funded Title 19 Program offer financial assistance to people who participate.
2. This assistance can run from reimbursement for your travel expenses to an actual salary for certain kinds of work.

Conclusion

[Action] I. I am urging you to volunteer time to help needy elderly people remain independent in their homes.
II. Spending time with elderly people living alone can help them meet their physical and emotional needs.
III. You can adjust the time you spend to fit your schedule, you can get great personal gratification from volunteering, and you can receive monetary benefits as well.
IV. But most important, Loretta Olson—and millions like her—will be forever thankful for your efforts.

PERSUASIVE SPEECH SELF-ASSESSMENT

Your task is to review your persuasive speech and to reach a full, objective assessment of its major strengths and weaknesses. Write a thoughtful evaluation of the speech in full-sentence and paragraph form with an introduction and a conclusion.

Be specific and concrete in your comments. Note in particular the areas in which you believe you did especially well and those areas in which you want to make special improvement in the next speech. Explain why you had difficulty with certain aspects of this speech and indicate the specific steps you will take to improve your next presentation.

Use the following questions to guide your self-assessment, though you do not need to answer each question individually in your paper. Be specific and concrete in your comments.

Topic and Purpose
    Was the topic appropriate for the audience and occasion?
    Did you have a clear specific purpose that you could accomplish in the allotted time?

Organization
    Was the speech well organized?
    Did you fulfill all the major functions of a speech introduction?
    Did you fulfill all the major objectives of a speech conclusion?
    Were the main points of the body clear and easy to follow?
    Did you use connectives effectively?

Supporting Materials, Audience Adaptation, and Language
    Did you conduct adequate research when preparing the speech?
    Were your ideas well supported and explained?
    If you spoke on a question of policy, did you demonstrate a need to change current policy?
    Did you present a clear plan to solve the need? Did you prove the practicality of your plan?
    Did you follow the criteria in your textbook for the effective use of supporting materials?
    Did you identify the target audience for your speech?
    Did you use evidence to answer the potential objections of your target audience?
    Did you present your ideas in clear, vivid, accurate, and appropriate language?

Delivery and Visual Aids
    Did you begin and end your speech without rushing?
    Did you use pauses, rate, pitch, and vocal variety effectively in delivering the speech?
    Did your nonverbal communication add to or detract from the speech?
    Did you maintain strong eye contact throughout the speech?
    If you used visual aids, were they carefully prepared and smoothly integrated into the speech?
    Did you follow the guidelines in your textbook for presenting visual aids?

Overall Assessment
    What were you most pleased with in the speech? What were you least pleased with?
    If you had an opportunity to deliver this speech again next week, what changes would you make? Be specific.

OUT-OF-CLASS OBSERVATION FOR A
SPEECH OF INTRODUCTION

Your name _____

Name of speaker you observed _____

Where was the speech presented? _____

Who was the speaker introducing? _____

Evaluate the speech of introduction as follows:

1. How long was the speech? Was it too long? Too short? About right? Explain.

2. As far as you can tell, was the speech accurate in its remarks about the main speaker? Explain.

3. Was the speech well adapted to the occasion? Explain.

4. Was the speech well adapted to the main speaker? Explain.

5. Was the speech well adapted to the audience? Explain.

6. Did the speech create a sense of anticipation and drama about the main speaker? Explain.

SPECIAL-OCCASION SPEECH SELF-ASSESSMENT

Your task is to review your special-occasion speech and to reach a full, objective assessment of its major strengths and weaknesses. Write a thoughtful, objective evaluation of the speech in full-sentence and paragraph form with an introduction and a conclusion.

Be specific and concrete in your comments. Note in particular the areas in which you believe you did especially well and those areas in which you want to make special improvement in the next speech. Explain why you had difficulty with certain aspects of this speech, and indicate the specific steps you plan to take to improve your next presentation.

Use the following questions to guide your self-assessment, though you do not need to answer each question individually in your paper. Be specific and concrete in your comments.

Topic
- Was the topic appropriate for the occasion?
- Was the topic appropriate for the audience?
- Did you deal with the topic creatively?

Organization
- Did your introduction gain the attention and interest of the audience?
- Were the main ideas of the speech easy to follow?
- Did you use connectives effectively?
- Did you conclude the speech in a memorable fashion?

Language
- Was your language clear and concrete?
- Was your language vivid and colorful?
- Was your language appropriate to the topic, audience, and occasion?

Delivery
- Did you begin and end your speech without rushing?
- Did you use pauses, rate, pitch, and vocal variety effectively in delivering the speech?
- Did your nonverbal communication add to or detract from the speech?
- Did you maintain strong eye contact throughout the speech?

Overall Assessment
- What were you most pleased with in the speech? What were you least pleased with?
- If you had an opportunity to deliver this speech again next week, what changes would you make? Be specific.

REFLECTIVE-THINKING METHOD CHECKLIST

		Yes	No
1.	Did the group clearly define the problem for discussion?	☐	☐
2.	Did the group phrase the question for discussion as a question of policy?	☐	☐
3.	Did the group phrase the question for discussion as clearly as possible?	☐	☐
4.	Did the group phrase the question for discussion so as to allow for a wide variety of answers?	☐	☐
5.	Did the group phrase the question for discussion in an unbiased manner?	☐	☐
6.	Did the group phrase the question for discussion as a single question?	☐	☐
7.	Did the group analyze the problem thoroughly before attempting to map out solutions?	☐	☐
8.	Did the group establish criteria for an ideal solution to the problem before discussing specific solutions?	☐	☐
9.	Did the group brainstorm to generate a wide range of potential solutions to the problem?	☐	☐
10.	Did the group evaluate each potential solution in light of the criteria for an ideal solution?	☐	☐
11.	Did the group make a determined effort to reach consensus with regard to the best solution?	☐	☐
12.	Did the group achieve consensus?	☐	☐

GROUP DISCUSSION SELF-ASSESSMENT

Your task is to reach a full, objective assessment of the major strengths and weaknesses of your small group and of your performance in the group. Write a thoughtful, objective evaluation in full-sentence and paragraph form with an introduction and a conclusion.

Use the following questions to guide your self-assessment, though you do not need to answer each question individually in your paper. Be specific and concrete in your comments.

Leadership
- Did your group have a designated leader?
- If you did not have a designated leader, what kind of leadership developed in the group?
- Which members were most effective in meeting the group's procedural needs?
- Which members were most effective in meeting the group's task needs?
- Which members were most effective in meeting the group's maintenance needs?

Responsibilities of Group Members
- How fully did members commit themselves to the goals of the group?
- How well did members carry out their individual assignments?
- Did the group avoid interpersonal conflict by keeping disagreement at the task level?
- Did vocal members encourage full participation by other members of the group?
- Did group members work to keep discussion on track?

Use of the Reflective-Thinking Method
- Did the group define the question for discussion clearly?
- Did the group analyze the problem thoroughly before attempting to map out solutions?
- Did the group establish criteria for an ideal solution?
- Did the group brainstorm to generate a wide range of potential solutions?
- Did the group evaluate each potential solution in light of the criteria for an ideal solution?
- Did the group make a determined effort to reach consensus about the best solution?
- Did the group achieve consensus? Why or why not?

Overall Evaluation
- Are you satisfied with the work of the group and with your role in the group?
- If the group were to start its project over again, what changes would you recommend to help the group work more effectively? Be specific.

SPEECH EVALUATION

FORMS

SPEECH EVALUATION FORM

Speaker _____

Topic _____

Rate the speaker on each point: E-excellent   G-good   A-average   F-fair   P-poor

INTRODUCTION
Gained attention and interest	E G A F P
Introduced topic clearly	E G A F P
Related topic to audience	E G A F P
Established credibility	E G A F P
Previewed body of speech	E G A F P

BODY
Main points clear	E G A F P
Main points fully supported	E G A F P
Organization well planned	E G A F P
Language accurate	E G A F P
Language clear	E G A F P
Language appropriate	E G A F P
Connectives effective	E G A F P

CONCLUSION
Prepared audience for ending	E G A F P
Reinforced central idea	E G A F P
Vivid ending	E G A F P

DELIVERY
Began speech without rushing	E G A F P
Maintained strong eye contact	E G A F P
Avoided distracting mannerisms	E G A F P
Articulated words clearly	E G A F P
Used pauses effectively	E G A F P
Used vocal variety to add impact	E G A F P
Presented visual aids well	E G A F P
Communicated enthusiasm for topic	E G A F P
Departed from lectern without rushing	E G A F P

OVERALL EVALUATION
Met assignment	E G A F P
Topic challenging	E G A F P
Specific purpose well chosen	E G A F P
Message adapted to audience	E G A F P
Speech completed within time limit	E G A F P
Held interest of audience	E G A F P

_____

What did the speaker do most effectively? _____

_____

What should the speaker pay special attention to next time? _____

_____

General Comments: _____

_____

SPEECH EVALUATION FORM

Speaker _____

Topic _____

Rate the speaker on each point: E-excellent   G-good   A-average   F-fair   P-poor

INTRODUCTION		**DELIVERY**	
Gained attention and interest	E G A F P	Began speech without rushing	E G A F P
Introduced topic clearly	E G A F P	Maintained strong eye contact	E G A F P
Related topic to audience	E G A F P	Avoided distracting mannerisms	E G A F P
Established credibility	E G A F P	Articulated words clearly	E G A F P
Previewed body of speech	E G A F P	Used pauses effectively	E G A F P
		Used vocal variety to add impact	E G A F P
BODY		Presented visual aids well	E G A F P
Main points clear	E G A F P	Communicated enthusiasm for topic	E G A F P
Main points fully supported	E G A F P	Departed from lectern without rushing	E G A F P
Organization well planned	E G A F P		
Language accurate	E G A F P	**OVERALL EVALUATION**	
Language clear	E G A F P	Met assignment	E G A F P
Language appropriate	E G A F P	Topic challenging	E G A F P
Connectives effective	E G A F P	Specific purpose well chosen	E G A F P
		Message adapted to audience	E G A F P
CONCLUSION		Speech completed within time limit	E G A F P
Prepared audience for ending	E G A F P	Held interest of audience	E G A F P
Reinforced central idea	E G A F P		
Vivid ending	E G A F P		

What did the speaker do most effectively? _____

_____

What should the speaker pay special attention to next time? _____

_____

General Comments: _____

_____

The Art of Public Speaking Workbook   73

SPEECH EVALUATION FORM

Speaker _____

Topic _____

Rate the speaker on each point: E-excellent   G-good   A-average   F-fair   P-poor

INTRODUCTION
Gained attention and interest	E G A F P
Introduced topic clearly	E G A F P
Related topic to audience	E G A F P
Established credibility	E G A F P
Previewed body of speech	E G A F P

BODY
Main points clear	E G A F P
Main points fully supported	E G A F P
Organization well planned	E G A F P
Language accurate	E G A F P
Language clear	E G A F P
Language appropriate	E G A F P
Connectives effective	E G A F P

CONCLUSION
Prepared audience for ending	E G A F P
Reinforced central idea	E G A F P
Vivid ending	E G A F P

DELIVERY
Began speech without rushing	E G A F P
Maintained strong eye contact	E G A F P
Avoided distracting mannerisms	E G A F P
Articulated words clearly	E G A F P
Used pauses effectively	E G A F P
Used vocal variety to add impact	E G A F P
Presented visual aids well	E G A F P
Communicated enthusiasm for topic	E G A F P
Departed from lectern without rushing	E G A F P

OVERALL EVALUATION
Met assignment	E G A F P
Topic challenging	E G A F P
Specific purpose well chosen	E G A F P
Message adapted to audience	E G A F P
Speech completed within time limit	E G A F P
Held interest of audience	E G A F P

What did the speaker do most effectively? _____

_____

_____

What should the speaker pay special attention to next time? _____

_____

_____

General Comments: _____

_____

_____

SPEECH EVALUATION FORM

Speaker _____

Topic _____

Rate the speaker on each point: E-excellent   G-good   A-average   F-fair   P-poor

INTRODUCTION
Gained attention and interest	E G A F P
Introduced topic clearly	E G A F P
Related topic to audience	E G A F P
Established credibility	E G A F P
Previewed body of speech	E G A F P

BODY
Main points clear	E G A F P
Main points fully supported	E G A F P
Organization well planned	E G A F P
Language accurate	E G A F P
Language clear	E G A F P
Language appropriate	E G A F P
Connectives effective	E G A F P

CONCLUSION
Prepared audience for ending	E G A F P
Reinforced central idea	E G A F P
Vivid ending	E G A F P

DELIVERY
Began speech without rushing	E G A F P
Maintained strong eye contact	E G A F P
Avoided distracting mannerisms	E G A F P
Articulated words clearly	E G A F P
Used pauses effectively	E G A F P
Used vocal variety to add impact	E G A F P
Presented visual aids well	E G A F P
Communicated enthusiasm for topic	E G A F P
Departed from lectern without rushing	E G A F P

OVERALL EVALUATION
Met assignment	E G A F P
Topic challenging	E G A F P
Specific purpose well chosen	E G A F P
Message adapted to audience	E G A F P
Speech completed within time limit	E G A F P
Held interest of audience	E G A F P

What did the speaker do most effectively? _____

What should the speaker pay special attention to next time? _____

General Comments: _____

SPEECH EVALUATION FORM

Speaker _____

Topic _____

Rate the speaker on each point: *E-excellent*   *G-good*   *A-average*   *F-fair*   *P-poor*

INTRODUCTION		DELIVERY	
Gained attention and interest	E G A F P	Began speech without rushing	E G A F P
Introduced topic clearly	E G A F P	Maintained strong eye contact	E G A F P
Related topic to audience	E G A F P	Avoided distracting mannerisms	E G A F P
Established credibility	E G A F P	Articulated words clearly	E G A F P
Previewed body of speech	E G A F P	Used pauses effectively	E G A F P
		Used vocal variety to add impact	E G A F P
BODY		Presented visual aids well	E G A F P
Main points clear	E G A F P	Communicated enthusiasm for topic	E G A F P
Main points fully supported	E G A F P	Departed from lectern without rushing	E G A F P
Organization well planned	E G A F P		
Language accurate	E G A F P	**OVERALL EVALUATION**	
Language clear	E G A F P	Met assignment	E G A F P
Language appropriate	E G A F P	Topic challenging	E G A F P
Connectives effective	E G A F P	Specific purpose well chosen	E G A F P
		Message adapted to audience	E G A F P
CONCLUSION		Speech completed within time limit	E G A F P
Prepared audience for ending	E G A F P	Held interest of audience	E G A F P
Reinforced central idea	E G A F P		
Vivid ending	E G A F P		

_____

What did the speaker do most effectively? _____

_____

What should the speaker pay special attention to next time? _____

_____

General Comments: _____

_____

SPEECH EVALUATION FORM

Speaker _____

Topic _____

Rate the speaker on each point: E-excellent   G-good   A-average   F-fair   P-poor

INTRODUCTION		**DELIVERY**	
Gained attention and interest	E G A F P	Began speech without rushing	E G A F P
Introduced topic clearly	E G A F P	Maintained strong eye contact	E G A F P
Related topic to audience	E G A F P	Avoided distracting mannerisms	E G A F P
Established credibility	E G A F P	Articulated words clearly	E G A F P
Previewed body of speech	E G A F P	Used pauses effectively	E G A F P
		Used vocal variety to add impact	E G A F P
BODY		Presented visual aids well	E G A F P
Main points clear	E G A F P	Communicated enthusiasm for topic	E G A F P
Main points fully supported	E G A F P	Departed from lectern without rushing	E G A F P
Organization well planned	E G A F P		
Language accurate	E G A F P	**OVERALL EVALUATION**	
Language clear	E G A F P	Met assignment	E G A F P
Language appropriate	E G A F P	Topic challenging	E G A F P
Connectives effective	E G A F P	Specific purpose well chosen	E G A F P
		Message adapted to audience	E G A F P
CONCLUSION		Speech completed within time limit	E G A F P
Prepared audience for ending	E G A F P	Held interest of audience	E G A F P
Reinforced central idea	E G A F P		
Vivid ending	E G A F P		

_____

What did the speaker do most effectively? _____

_____

What should the speaker pay special attention to next time? _____

_____

General Comments: _____

_____

SPEECH EVALUATION FORM

Speaker _____

Topic _____

Rate the speaker on each point: *E-excellent*   *G-good*   *A-average*   *F-fair*   *P-poor*

INTRODUCTION		DELIVERY	
Gained attention and interest	E G A F P	Began speech without rushing	E G A F P
Introduced topic clearly	E G A F P	Maintained strong eye contact	E G A F P
Related topic to audience	E G A F P	Avoided distracting mannerisms	E G A F P
Established credibility	E G A F P	Articulated words clearly	E G A F P
Previewed body of speech	E G A F P	Used pauses effectively	E G A F P
		Used vocal variety to add impact	E G A F P
BODY		Presented visual aids well	E G A F P
Main points clear	E G A F P	Communicated enthusiasm for topic	E G A F P
Main points fully supported	E G A F P	Departed from lectern without rushing	E G A F P
Organization well planned	E G A F P		
Language accurate	E G A F P	**OVERALL EVALUATION**	
Language clear	E G A F P	Met assignment	E G A F P
Language appropriate	E G A F P	Topic challenging	E G A F P
Connectives effective	E G A F P	Specific purpose well chosen	E G A F P
		Message adapted to audience	E G A F P
CONCLUSION		Speech completed within time limit	E G A F P
Prepared audience for ending	E G A F P	Held interest of audience	E G A F P
Reinforced central idea	E G A F P		
Vivid ending	E G A F P		

_____

What did the speaker do most effectively? _____

_____

_____

What should the speaker pay special attention to next time? _____

_____

_____

General Comments: _____

_____

_____

_____

SPEECH EVALUATION FORM

Speaker _____

Topic _____

Rate the speaker on each point: *E-excellent*   *G-good*   *A-average*   *F-fair*   *P-poor*

INTRODUCTION
Gained attention and interest   E G A F P
Introduced topic clearly   E G A F P
Related topic to audience   E G A F P
Established credibility   E G A F P
Previewed body of speech   E G A F P

BODY
Main points clear   E G A F P
Main points fully supported   E G A F P
Organization well planned   E G A F P
Language accurate   E G A F P
Language clear   E G A F P
Language appropriate   E G A F P
Connectives effective   E G A F P

CONCLUSION
Prepared audience for ending   E G A F P
Reinforced central idea   E G A F P
Vivid ending   E G A F P

DELIVERY
Began speech without rushing   E G A F P
Maintained strong eye contact   E G A F P
Avoided distracting mannerisms   E G A F P
Articulated words clearly   E G A F P
Used pauses effectively   E G A F P
Used vocal variety to add impact   E G A F P
Presented visual aids well   E G A F P
Communicated enthusiasm for topic   E G A F P
Departed from lectern without rushing   E G A F P

OVERALL EVALUATION
Met assignment   E G A F P
Topic challenging   E G A F P
Specific purpose well chosen   E G A F P
Message adapted to audience   E G A F P
Speech completed within time limit   E G A F P
Held interest of audience   E G A F P

_____

What did the speaker do most effectively? _____

_____

What should the speaker pay special attention to next time? _____

_____

General Comments: _____

_____

SPEECH EVALUATION FORM

Speaker _____

Topic _____

Rate the speaker on each point: E-excellent   G-good   A-average   F-fair   P-poor

INTRODUCTION		**DELIVERY**	
Gained attention and interest	E G A F P	Began speech without rushing	E G A F P
Introduced topic clearly	E G A F P	Maintained strong eye contact	E G A F P
Related topic to audience	E G A F P	Avoided distracting mannerisms	E G A F P
Established credibility	E G A F P	Articulated words clearly	E G A F P
Previewed body of speech	E G A F P	Used pauses effectively	E G A F P
		Used vocal variety to add impact	E G A F P
BODY		Presented visual aids well	E G A F P
Main points clear	E G A F P	Communicated enthusiasm for topic	E G A F P
Main points fully supported	E G A F P	Departed from lectern without rushing	E G A F P
Organization well planned	E G A F P		
Language accurate	E G A F P	**OVERALL EVALUATION**	
Language clear	E G A F P	Met assignment	E G A F P
Language appropriate	E G A F P	Topic challenging	E G A F P
Connectives effective	E G A F P	Specific purpose well chosen	E G A F P
		Message adapted to audience	E G A F P
CONCLUSION		Speech completed within time limit	E G A F P
Prepared audience for ending	E G A F P	Held interest of audience	E G A F P
Reinforced central idea	E G A F P		
Vivid ending	E G A F P		

What did the speaker do most effectively? _____

_____

What should the speaker pay special attention to next time? _____

_____

_____

General Comments: _____

_____

_____

_____

SPEECH EVALUATION FORM

Speaker _____

Topic _____

Rate the speaker on each point: E-excellent   G-good   A-average   F-fair   P-poor

INTRODUCTION		**DELIVERY**	
Gained attention and interest	E G A F P	Began speech without rushing	E G A F P
Introduced topic clearly	E G A F P	Maintained strong eye contact	E G A F P
Related topic to audience	E G A F P	Avoided distracting mannerisms	E G A F P
Established credibility	E G A F P	Articulated words clearly	E G A F P
Previewed body of speech	E G A F P	Used pauses effectively	E G A F P
		Used vocal variety to add impact	E G A F P
BODY		Presented visual aids well	E G A F P
Main points clear	E G A F P	Communicated enthusiasm for topic	E G A F P
Main points fully supported	E G A F P	Departed from lectern without rushing	E G A F P
Organization well planned	E G A F P		
Language accurate	E G A F P	**OVERALL EVALUATION**	
Language clear	E G A F P	Met assignment	E G A F P
Language appropriate	E G A F P	Topic challenging	E G A F P
Connectives effective	E G A F P	Specific purpose well chosen	E G A F P
		Message adapted to audience	E G A F P
CONCLUSION		Speech completed within time limit	E G A F P
Prepared audience for ending	E G A F P	Held interest of audience	E G A F P
Reinforced central idea	E G A F P		
Vivid ending	E G A F P		

_____

What did the speaker do most effectively? _____

_____

_____

What should the speaker pay special attention to next time? _____

_____

_____

General Comments: _____

_____

_____

_____

SPEECH EVALUATION FORM

Speaker _____

Topic _____

Rate the speaker on each point: *E-excellent*   *G-good*   *A-average*   *F-fair*   *P-poor*

INTRODUCTION		**DELIVERY**	
Gained attention and interest	E G A F P	Began speech without rushing	E G A F P
Introduced topic clearly	E G A F P	Maintained strong eye contact	E G A F P
Related topic to audience	E G A F P	Avoided distracting mannerisms	E G A F P
Established credibility	E G A F P	Articulated words clearly	E G A F P
Previewed body of speech	E G A F P	Used pauses effectively	E G A F P
		Used vocal variety to add impact	E G A F P
BODY		Presented visual aids well	E G A F P
Main points clear	E G A F P	Communicated enthusiasm for topic	E G A F P
Main points fully supported	E G A F P	Departed from lectern without rushing	E G A F P
Organization well planned	E G A F P		
Language accurate	E G A F P	**OVERALL EVALUATION**	
Language clear	E G A F P	Met assignment	E G A F P
Language appropriate	E G A F P	Topic challenging	E G A F P
Connectives effective	E G A F P	Specific purpose well chosen	E G A F P
		Message adapted to audience	E G A F P
CONCLUSION		Speech completed within time limit	E G A F P
Prepared audience for ending	E G A F P	Held interest of audience	E G A F P
Reinforced central idea	E G A F P		
Vivid ending	E G A F P		

_____

What did the speaker do most effectively? _____

_____

What should the speaker pay special attention to next time? _____

_____

General Comments: _____

_____

SPEECH EVALUATION FORM

Speaker _____

Topic _____

Rate the speaker on each point: E-excellent G-good A-average F-fair P-poor

INTRODUCTION		DELIVERY	
Gained attention and interest	E G A F P	Began speech without rushing	E G A F P
Introduced topic clearly	E G A F P	Maintained strong eye contact	E G A F P
Related topic to audience	E G A F P	Avoided distracting mannerisms	E G A F P
Established credibility	E G A F P	Articulated words clearly	E G A F P
Previewed body of speech	E G A F P	Used pauses effectively	E G A F P
		Used vocal variety to add impact	E G A F P
BODY		Presented visual aids well	E G A F P
Main points clear	E G A F P	Communicated enthusiasm for topic	E G A F P
Main points fully supported	E G A F P	Departed from lectern without rushing	E G A F P
Organization well planned	E G A F P		
Language accurate	E G A F P	**OVERALL EVALUATION**	
Language clear	E G A F P	Met assignment	E G A F P
Language appropriate	E G A F P	Topic challenging	E G A F P
Connectives effective	E G A F P	Specific purpose well chosen	E G A F P
		Message adapted to audience	E G A F P
CONCLUSION		Speech completed within time limit	E G A F P
Prepared audience for ending	E G A F P	Held interest of audience	E G A F P
Reinforced central idea	E G A F P		
Vivid ending	E G A F P		

_____

What did the speaker do most effectively? _____

_____

What should the speaker pay special attention to next time? ___

_____

General Comments: _____

_____

SPEECH EVALUATION FORM

Speaker _____

Topic _____

Rate the speaker on each point: E-*excellent*   G-*good*   A-*average*   F-*fair*   P-*poor*

INTRODUCTION		**DELIVERY**	
Gained attention and interest	E G A F P	Began speech without rushing	E G A F P
Introduced topic clearly	E G A F P	Maintained strong eye contact	E G A F P
Related topic to audience	E G A F P	Avoided distracting mannerisms	E G A F P
Established credibility	E G A F P	Articulated words clearly	E G A F P
Previewed body of speech	E G A F P	Used pauses effectively	E G A F P
		Used vocal variety to add impact	E G A F P
BODY		Presented visual aids well	E G A F P
Main points clear	E G A F P	Communicated enthusiasm for topic	E G A F P
Main points fully supported	E G A F P	Departed from lectern without rushing	E G A F P
Organization well planned	E G A F P		
Language accurate	E G A F P	**OVERALL EVALUATION**	
Language clear	E G A F P	Met assignment	E G A F P
Language appropriate	E G A F P	Topic challenging	E G A F P
Connectives effective	E G A F P	Specific purpose well chosen	E G A F P
		Message adapted to audience	E G A F P
CONCLUSION		Speech completed within time limit	E G A F P
Prepared audience for ending	E G A F P	Held interest of audience	E G A F P
Reinforced central idea	E G A F P		
Vivid ending	E G A F P		

_____

What did the speaker do most effectively? _____

_____

_____

What should the speaker pay special attention to next time? _____

_____

_____

General Comments: _____

_____

_____

_____

SPEECH EVALUATION FORM

Speaker _____

Topic _____

Rate the speaker on each point: *E-excellent*   *G-good*   *A-average*   *F-fair*   *P-poor*

INTRODUCTION		DELIVERY	
Gained attention and interest	E G A F P	Began speech without rushing	E G A F P
Introduced topic clearly	E G A F P	Maintained strong eye contact	E G A F P
Related topic to audience	E G A F P	Avoided distracting mannerisms	E G A F P
Established credibility	E G A F P	Articulated words clearly	E G A F P
Previewed body of speech	E G A F P	Used pauses effectively	E G A F P
		Used vocal variety to add impact	E G A F P
BODY		Presented visual aids well	E G A F P
Main points clear	E G A F P	Communicated enthusiasm for topic	E G A F P
Main points fully supported	E G A F P	Departed from lectern without rushing	E G A F P
Organization well planned	E G A F P		
Language accurate	E G A F P	**OVERALL EVALUATION**	
Language clear	E G A F P	Met assignment	E G A F P
Language appropriate	E G A F P	Topic challenging	E G A F P
Connectives effective	E G A F P	Specific purpose well chosen	E G A F P
		Message adapted to audience	E G A F P
CONCLUSION		Speech completed within time limit	E G A F P
Prepared audience for ending	E G A F P	Held interest of audience	E G A F P
Reinforced central idea	E G A F P		
Vivid ending	E G A F P		

_____

What did the speaker do most effectively? _____

_____

_____

What should the speaker pay special attention to next time? ___

_____

_____

General Comments: _____

_____

_____

_____

SPEECH EVALUATION FORM

Speaker _____

Topic _____

Rate the speaker on each point: *E-excellent*   *G-good*   *A-average*   *F-fair*   *P-poor*

INTRODUCTION
Gained attention and interest	E G A F P
Introduced topic clearly	E G A F P
Related topic to audience	E G A F P
Established credibility	E G A F P
Previewed body of speech	E G A F P

BODY
Main points clear	E G A F P
Main points fully supported	E G A F P
Organization well planned	E G A F P
Language accurate	E G A F P
Language clear	E G A F P
Language appropriate	E G A F P
Connectives effective	E G A F P

CONCLUSION
Prepared audience for ending	E G A F P
Reinforced central idea	E G A F P
Vivid ending	E G A F P

DELIVERY
Began speech without rushing	E G A F P
Maintained strong eye contact	E G A F P
Avoided distracting mannerisms	E G A F P
Articulated words clearly	E G A F P
Used pauses effectively	E G A F P
Used vocal variety to add impact	E G A F P
Presented visual aids well	E G A F P
Communicated enthusiasm for topic	E G A F P
Departed from lectern without rushing	E G A F P

OVERALL EVALUATION
Met assignment	E G A F P
Topic challenging	E G A F P
Specific purpose well chosen	E G A F P
Message adapted to audience	E G A F P
Speech completed within time limit	E G A F P
Held interest of audience	E G A F P

What did the speaker do most effectively? _____

What should the speaker pay special attention to next time? _____

General Comments: _____

SPEECH EVALUATION FORM

Speaker _____

Topic _____

Rate the speaker on each point: *E-excellent*   *G-good*   *A-average*   *F-fair*   *P-poor*

INTRODUCTION
Gained attention and interest   E G A F P
Introduced topic clearly   E G A F P
Related topic to audience   E G A F P
Established credibility   E G A F P
Previewed body of speech   E G A F P

BODY
Main points clear   E G A F P
Main points fully supported   E G A F P
Organization well planned   E G A F P
Language accurate   E G A F P
Language clear   E G A F P
Language appropriate   E G A F P
Connectives effective   E G A F P

CONCLUSION
Prepared audience for ending   E G A F P
Reinforced central idea   E G A F P
Vivid ending   E G A F P

DELIVERY
Began speech without rushing   E G A F P
Maintained strong eye contact   E G A F P
Avoided distracting mannerisms   E G A F P
Articulated words clearly   E G A F P
Used pauses effectively   E G A F P
Used vocal variety to add impact   E G A F P
Presented visual aids well   E G A F P
Communicated enthusiasm for topic   E G A F P
Departed from lectern without rushing E G A F P

OVERALL EVALUATION
Met assignment   E G A F P
Topic challenging   E G A F P
Specific purpose well chosen   E G A F P
Message adapted to audience   E G A F P
Speech completed within time limit E G A F P
Held interest of audience   E G A F P

_____

What did the speaker do most effectively? _____

_____

_____

What should the speaker pay special attention to next time? _____

_____

_____

General Comments: _____

_____

_____

_____

SPEECH EVALUATION FORM

Speaker _____

Topic _____

Rate the speaker on each point: E-excellent   G-good   A-average   F-fair   P-poor

INTRODUCTION		**DELIVERY**	
Gained attention and interest	E G A F P	Began speech without rushing	E G A F P
Introduced topic clearly	E G A F P	Maintained strong eye contact	E G A F P
Related topic to audience	E G A F P	Avoided distracting mannerisms	E G A F P
Established credibility	E G A F P	Articulated words clearly	E G A F P
Previewed body of speech	E G A F P	Used pauses effectively	E G A F P
		Used vocal variety to add impact	E G A F P
BODY		Presented visual aids well	E G A F P
Main points clear	E G A F P	Communicated enthusiasm for topic	E G A F P
Main points fully supported	E G A F P	Departed from lectern without rushing	E G A F P
Organization well planned	E G A F P		
Language accurate	E G A F P	**OVERALL EVALUATION**	
Language clear	E G A F P	Met assignment	E G A F P
Language appropriate	E G A F P	Topic challenging	E G A F P
Connectives effective	E G A F P	Specific purpose well chosen	E G A F P
		Message adapted to audience	E G A F P
CONCLUSION		Speech completed within time limit	E G A F P
Prepared audience for ending	E G A F P	Held interest of audience	E G A F P
Reinforced central idea	E G A F P		
Vivid ending	E G A F P		

What did the speaker do most effectively? _____
_____

What should the speaker pay special attention to next time? _____
_____

General Comments: _____
_____

SPEECH EVALUATION FORM

Speaker _____

Topic _____

Rate the speaker on each point: E-excellent   G-good   A-average   F-fair   P-poor

INTRODUCTION
Gained attention and interest	E G A F P
Introduced topic clearly	E G A F P
Related topic to audience	E G A F P
Established credibility	E G A F P
Previewed body of speech	E G A F P

BODY
Main points clear	E G A F P
Main points fully supported	E G A F P
Organization well planned	E G A F P
Language accurate	E G A F P
Language clear	E G A F P
Language appropriate	E G A F P
Connectives effective	E G A F P

CONCLUSION
Prepared audience for ending	E G A F P
Reinforced central idea	E G A F P
Vivid ending	E G A F P

DELIVERY
Began speech without rushing	E G A F P
Maintained strong eye contact	E G A F P
Avoided distracting mannerisms	E G A F P
Articulated words clearly	E G A F P
Used pauses effectively	E G A F P
Used vocal variety to add impact	E G A F P
Presented visual aids well	E G A F P
Communicated enthusiasm for topic	E G A F P
Departed from lectern without rushing	E G A F P

OVERALL EVALUATION
Met assignment	E G A F P
Topic challenging	E G A F P
Specific purpose well chosen	E G A F P
Message adapted to audience	E G A F P
Speech completed within time limit	E G A F P
Held interest of audience	E G A F P

_____

What did the speaker do most effectively? _____

What should the speaker pay special attention to next time? _____

General Comments: _____

SPEECH EVALUATION FORM

Speaker _____

Topic _____

Rate the speaker on each point: E-*excellent*   G-*good*   A-*average*   F-*fair*   P-*poor*

INTRODUCTION		**DELIVERY**	
Gained attention and interest	E G A F P	Began speech without rushing	E G A F P
Introduced topic clearly	E G A F P	Maintained strong eye contact	E G A F P
Related topic to audience	E G A F P	Avoided distracting mannerisms	E G A F P
Established credibility	E G A F P	Articulated words clearly	E G A F P
Previewed body of speech	E G A F P	Used pauses effectively	E G A F P
		Used vocal variety to add impact	E G A F P
BODY		Presented visual aids well	E G A F P
Main points clear	E G A F P	Communicated enthusiasm for topic	E G A F P
Main points fully supported	E G A F P	Departed from lectern without rushing	E G A F P
Organization well planned	E G A F P		
Language accurate	E G A F P	**OVERALL EVALUATION**	
Language clear	E G A F P	Met assignment	E G A F P
Language appropriate	E G A F P	Topic challenging	E G A F P
Connectives effective	E G A F P	Specific purpose well chosen	E G A F P
		Message adapted to audience	E G A F P
CONCLUSION		Speech completed within time limit	E G A F P
Prepared audience for ending	E G A F P	Held interest of audience	E G A F P
Reinforced central idea	E G A F P		
Vivid ending	E G A F P		

What did the speaker do most effectively? _____

_____

_____

What should the speaker pay special attention to next time? _____

_____

_____

General Comments: _____

_____

_____

SPEECH EVALUATION FORM

Speaker _____

Topic _____

Rate the speaker on each point: *E-excellent*   *G-good*   *A-average*   *F-fair*   *P-poor*

INTRODUCTION		**DELIVERY**	
Gained attention and interest	E G A F P	Began speech without rushing	E G A F P
Introduced topic clearly	E G A F P	Maintained strong eye contact	E G A F P
Related topic to audience	E G A F P	Avoided distracting mannerisms	E G A F P
Established credibility	E G A F P	Articulated words clearly	E G A F P
Previewed body of speech	E G A F P	Used pauses effectively	E G A F P
		Used vocal variety to add impact	E G A F P
BODY		Presented visual aids well	E G A F P
Main points clear	E G A F P	Communicated enthusiasm for topic	E G A F P
Main points fully supported	E G A F P	Departed from lectern without rushing	E G A F P
Organization well planned	E G A F P		
Language accurate	E G A F P	**OVERALL EVALUATION**	
Language clear	E G A F P	Met assignment	E G A F P
Language appropriate	E G A F P	Topic challenging	E G A F P
Connectives effective	E G A F P	Specific purpose well chosen	E G A F P
		Message adapted to audience	E G A F P
CONCLUSION		Speech completed within time limit	E G A F P
Prepared audience for ending	E G A F P	Held interest of audience	E G A F P
Reinforced central idea	E G A F P		
Vivid ending	E G A F P		

_____

What did the speaker do most effectively? _____

_____

What should the speaker pay special attention to next time? _____

_____

General Comments: _____

_____

SPEECH EVALUATION FORM

Speaker _____

Topic _____

Rate the speaker on each point: *E-excellent*   *G-good*   *A-average*   *F-fair*   *P-poor*

INTRODUCTION		DELIVERY	
Gained attention and interest	E G A F P	Began speech without rushing	E G A F P
Introduced topic clearly	E G A F P	Maintained strong eye contact	E G A F P
Related topic to audience	E G A F P	Avoided distracting mannerisms	E G A F P
Established credibility	E G A F P	Articulated words clearly	E G A F P
Previewed body of speech	E G A F P	Used pauses effectively	E G A F P
		Used vocal variety to add impact	E G A F P
BODY		Presented visual aids well	E G A F P
Main points clear	E G A F P	Communicated enthusiasm for topic	E G A F P
Main points fully supported	E G A F P	Departed from lectern without rushing	E G A F P
Organization well planned	E G A F P		
Language accurate	E G A F P	**OVERALL EVALUATION**	
Language clear	E G A F P	Met assignment	E G A F P
Language appropriate	E G A F P	Topic challenging	E G A F P
Connectives effective	E G A F P	Specific purpose well chosen	E G A F P
		Message adapted to audience	E G A F P
CONCLUSION		Speech completed within time limit	E G A F P
Prepared audience for ending	E G A F P	Held interest of audience	E G A F P
Reinforced central idea	E G A F P		
Vivid ending	E G A F P		

_____

What did the speaker do most effectively? _____

_____

What should the speaker pay special attention to next time? _____

_____

General Comments: _____

_____

SPEECH EVALUATION FORM

Speaker _____

Topic _____

Rate the speaker on each point: *E-excellent*   *G-good*   *A-average*   *F-fair*   *P-poor*

INTRODUCTION
Gained attention and interest	E G A F P
Introduced topic clearly	E G A F P
Related topic to audience	E G A F P
Established credibility	E G A F P
Previewed body of speech	E G A F P

BODY
Main points clear	E G A F P
Main points fully supported	E G A F P
Organization well planned	E G A F P
Language accurate	E G A F P
Language clear	E G A F P
Language appropriate	E G A F P
Connectives effective	E G A F P

CONCLUSION
Prepared audience for ending	E G A F P
Reinforced central idea	E G A F P
Vivid ending	E G A F P

DELIVERY
Began speech without rushing	E G A F P
Maintained strong eye contact	E G A F P
Avoided distracting mannerisms	E G A F P
Articulated words clearly	E G A F P
Used pauses effectively	E G A F P
Used vocal variety to add impact	E G A F P
Presented visual aids well	E G A F P
Communicated enthusiasm for topic	E G A F P
Departed from lectern without rushing	E G A F P

OVERALL EVALUATION
Met assignment	E G A F P
Topic challenging	E G A F P
Specific purpose well chosen	E G A F P
Message adapted to audience	E G A F P
Speech completed within time limit	E G A F P
Held interest of audience	E G A F P

_____

What did the speaker do most effectively? _____

_____

What should the speaker pay special attention to next time? _____

_____

General Comments: _____

SPEECH EVALUATION FORM

Speaker _____

Topic _____

Rate the speaker on each point: E-excellent   G-good   A-average   F-fair   P-poor

INTRODUCTION		DELIVERY	
Gained attention and interest	E G A F P	Began speech without rushing	E G A F P
Introduced topic clearly	E G A F P	Maintained strong eye contact	E G A F P
Related topic to audience	E G A F P	Avoided distracting mannerisms	E G A F P
Established credibility	E G A F P	Articulated words clearly	E G A F P
Previewed body of speech	E G A F P	Used pauses effectively	E G A F P
		Used vocal variety to add impact	E G A F P
BODY		Presented visual aids well	E G A F P
Main points clear	E G A F P	Communicated enthusiasm for topic	E G A F P
Main points fully supported	E G A F P	Departed from lectern without rushing	E G A F P
Organization well planned	E G A F P		
Language accurate	E G A F P	**OVERALL EVALUATION**	
Language clear	E G A F P	Met assignment	E G A F P
Language appropriate	E G A F P	Topic challenging	E G A F P
Connectives effective	E G A F P	Specific purpose well chosen	E G A F P
		Message adapted to audience	E G A F P
CONCLUSION		Speech completed within time limit	E G A F P
Prepared audience for ending	E G A F P	Held interest of audience	E G A F P
Reinforced central idea	E G A F P		
Vivid ending	E G A F P		

_____

What did the speaker do most effectively? _____

_____

_____

What should the speaker pay special attention to next time? _____

_____

_____

General Comments: _____

_____

_____

_____

SPEECH EVALUATION FORM

Speaker _____

Topic _____

Rate the speaker on each point: *E-excellent*   *G-good*   *A-average*   *F-fair*   *P-poor*

INTRODUCTION
Gained attention and interest   E G A F P
Introduced topic clearly   E G A F P
Related topic to audience   E G A F P
Established credibility   E G A F P
Previewed body of speech   E G A F P

BODY
Main points clear   E G A F P
Main points fully supported   E G A F P
Organization well planned   E G A F P
Language accurate   E G A F P
Language clear   E G A F P
Language appropriate   E G A F P
Connectives effective   E G A F P

CONCLUSION
Prepared audience for ending   E G A F P
Reinforced central idea   E G A F P
Vivid ending   E G A F P

DELIVERY
Began speech without rushing   E G A F P
Maintained strong eye contact   E G A F P
Avoided distracting mannerisms   E G A F P
Articulated words clearly   E G A F P
Used pauses effectively   E G A F P
Used vocal variety to add impact   E G A F P
Presented visual aids well   E G A F P
Communicated enthusiasm for topic   E G A F P
Departed from lectern without rushing E G A F P

OVERALL EVALUATION
Met assignment   E G A F P
Topic challenging   E G A F P
Specific purpose well chosen   E G A F P
Message adapted to audience   E G A F P
Speech completed within time limit E G A F P
Held interest of audience   E G A F P

_____

What did the speaker do most effectively? _____

_____

What should the speaker pay special attention to next time? _____

_____

General Comments: _____

_____

SPEECH EVALUATION FORM

Speaker _____

Topic _____

Rate the speaker on each point: E-excellent   G-good   A-average   F-fair   P-poor

INTRODUCTION

Gained attention and interest	E G A F P
Introduced topic clearly	E G A F P
Related topic to audience	E G A F P
Established credibility	E G A F P
Previewed body of speech	E G A F P

BODY

Main points clear	E G A F P
Main points fully supported	E G A F P
Organization well planned	E G A F P
Language accurate	E G A F P
Language clear	E G A F P
Language appropriate	E G A F P
Connectives effective	E G A F P

CONCLUSION

Prepared audience for ending	E G A F P
Reinforced central idea	E G A F P
Vivid ending	E G A F P

DELIVERY

Began speech without rushing	E G A F P
Maintained strong eye contact	E G A F P
Avoided distracting mannerisms	E G A F P
Articulated words clearly	E G A F P
Used pauses effectively	E G A F P
Used vocal variety to add impact	E G A F P
Presented visual aids well	E G A F P
Communicated enthusiasm for topic	E G A F P
Departed from lectern without rushing	E G A F P

OVERALL EVALUATION

Met assignment	E G A F P
Topic challenging	E G A F P
Specific purpose well chosen	E G A F P
Message adapted to audience	E G A F P
Speech completed within time limit	E G A F P
Held interest of audience	E G A F P

_____

What did the speaker do most effectively? _____

_____

_____

What should the speaker pay special attention to next time? _____

_____

_____

General Comments: _____

_____

_____

_____

SPEECH EVALUATION FORM

Speaker _____

Topic _____

Rate the speaker on each point: *E-excellent*   *G-good*   *A-average*   *F-fair*   *P-poor*

INTRODUCTION		**DELIVERY**	
Gained attention and interest	E G A F P	Began speech without rushing	E G A F P
Introduced topic clearly	E G A F P	Maintained strong eye contact	E G A F P
Related topic to audience	E G A F P	Avoided distracting mannerisms	E G A F P
Established credibility	E G A F P	Articulated words clearly	E G A F P
Previewed body of speech	E G A F P	Used pauses effectively	E G A F P
		Used vocal variety to add impact	E G A F P
BODY		Presented visual aids well	E G A F P
Main points clear	E G A F P	Communicated enthusiasm for topic	E G A F P
Main points fully supported	E G A F P	Departed from lectern without rushing	E G A F P
Organization well planned	E G A F P		
Language accurate	E G A F P	**OVERALL EVALUATION**	
Language clear	E G A F P	Met assignment	E G A F P
Language appropriate	E G A F P	Topic challenging	E G A F P
Connectives effective	E G A F P	Specific purpose well chosen	E G A F P
		Message adapted to audience	E G A F P
CONCLUSION		Speech completed within time limit	E G A F P
Prepared audience for ending	E G A F P	Held interest of audience	E G A F P
Reinforced central idea	E G A F P		
Vivid ending	E G A F P		

_____

What did the speaker do most effectively? _____

_____

What should the speaker pay special attention to next time? _____

_____

General Comments: _____

_____

SPEECH EVALUATION FORM

Speaker _____

Topic _____

Rate the speaker on each point: *E-excellent*   *G-good*   *A-average*   *F-fair*   *P-poor*

INTRODUCTION		DELIVERY	
Gained attention and interest	E G A F P	Began speech without rushing	E G A F P
Introduced topic clearly	E G A F P	Maintained strong eye contact	E G A F P
Related topic to audience	E G A F P	Avoided distracting mannerisms	E G A F P
Established credibility	E G A F P	Articulated words clearly	E G A F P
Previewed body of speech	E G A F P	Used pauses effectively	E G A F P
		Used vocal variety to add impact	E G A F P
BODY		Presented visual aids well	E G A F P
Main points clear	E G A F P	Communicated enthusiasm for topic	E G A F P
Main points fully supported	E G A F P	Departed from lectern without rushing	E G A F P
Organization well planned	E G A F P		
Language accurate	E G A F P	**OVERALL EVALUATION**	
Language clear	E G A F P	Met assignment	E G A F P
Language appropriate	E G A F P	Topic challenging	E G A F P
Connectives effective	E G A F P	Specific purpose well chosen	E G A F P
		Message adapted to audience	E G A F P
CONCLUSION		Speech completed within time limit	E G A F P
Prepared audience for ending	E G A F P	Held interest of audience	E G A F P
Reinforced central idea	E G A F P		
Vivid ending	E G A F P		

What did the speaker do most effectively? _____

_____

What should the speaker pay special attention to next time? _____

_____

General Comments: _____

_____

SPEECH EVALUATION FORM

Speaker _____

Topic _____

Rate the speaker on each point: *E-excellent*   *G-good*   *A-average*   *F-fair*   *P-poor*

INTRODUCTION		**DELIVERY**	
Gained attention and interest	E G A F P	Began speech without rushing	E G A F P
Introduced topic clearly	E G A F P	Maintained strong eye contact	E G A F P
Related topic to audience	E G A F P	Avoided distracting mannerisms	E G A F P
Established credibility	E G A F P	Articulated words clearly	E G A F P
Previewed body of speech	E G A F P	Used pauses effectively	E G A F P
		Used vocal variety to add impact	E G A F P
BODY		Presented visual aids well	E G A F P
Main points clear	E G A F P	Communicated enthusiasm for topic	E G A F P
Main points fully supported	E G A F P	Departed from lectern without rushing	E G A F P
Organization well planned	E G A F P		
Language accurate	E G A F P	**OVERALL EVALUATION**	
Language clear	E G A F P	Met assignment	E G A F P
Language appropriate	E G A F P	Topic challenging	E G A F P
Connectives effective	E G A F P	Specific purpose well chosen	E G A F P
		Message adapted to audience	E G A F P
CONCLUSION		Speech completed within time limit	E G A F P
Prepared audience for ending	E G A F P	Held interest of audience	E G A F P
Reinforced central idea	E G A F P		
Vivid ending	E G A F P		

_____

What did the speaker do most effectively? _____
_____
_____

What should the speaker pay special attention to next time? _____
_____
_____

General Comments: _____
_____
_____
_____

SPEECH EVALUATION FORM

Speaker _____

Topic _____

Rate the speaker on each point: *E-excellent*   *G-good*   *A-average*   *F-fair*   *P-poor*

INTRODUCTION
Gained attention and interest   E G A F P
Introduced topic clearly   E G A F P
Related topic to audience   E G A F P
Established credibility   E G A F P
Previewed body of speech   E G A F P

BODY
Main points clear   E G A F P
Main points fully supported   E G A F P
Organization well planned   E G A F P
Language accurate   E G A F P
Language clear   E G A F P
Language appropriate   E G A F P
Connectives effective   E G A F P

CONCLUSION
Prepared audience for ending   E G A F P
Reinforced central idea   E G A F P
Vivid ending   E G A F P

DELIVERY
Began speech without rushing   E G A F P
Maintained strong eye contact   E G A F P
Avoided distracting mannerisms   E G A F P
Articulated words clearly   E G A F P
Used pauses effectively   E G A F P
Used vocal variety to add impact   E G A F P
Presented visual aids well   E G A F P
Communicated enthusiasm for topic   E G A F P
Departed from lectern without rushing   E G A F P

OVERALL EVALUATION
Met assignment   E G A F P
Topic challenging   E G A F P
Specific purpose well chosen   E G A F P
Message adapted to audience   E G A F P
Speech completed within time limit   E G A F P
Held interest of audience   E G A F P

_____

What did the speaker do most effectively? _____
_____

What should the speaker pay special attention to next time? _____
_____

General Comments: _____
_____
_____
_____

SPEECH EVALUATION FORM

Speaker _____

Topic _____

Rate the speaker on each point: E-*excellent*   G-*good*   A-*average*   F-*fair*   P-*poor*

INTRODUCTION		DELIVERY	
Gained attention and interest	E G A F P	Began speech without rushing	E G A F P
Introduced topic clearly	E G A F P	Maintained strong eye contact	E G A F P
Related topic to audience	E G A F P	Avoided distracting mannerisms	E G A F P
Established credibility	E G A F P	Articulated words clearly	E G A F P
Previewed body of speech	E G A F P	Used pauses effectively	E G A F P
		Used vocal variety to add impact	E G A F P
BODY		Presented visual aids well	E G A F P
Main points clear	E G A F P	Communicated enthusiasm for topic	E G A F P
Main points fully supported	E G A F P	Departed from lectern without rushing	E G A F P
Organization well planned	E G A F P		
Language accurate	E G A F P	**OVERALL EVALUATION**	
Language clear	E G A F P	Met assignment	E G A F P
Language appropriate	E G A F P	Topic challenging	E G A F P
Connectives effective	E G A F P	Specific purpose well chosen	E G A F P
		Message adapted to audience	E G A F P
CONCLUSION		Speech completed within time limit	E G A F P
Prepared audience for ending	E G A F P	Held interest of audience	E G A F P
Reinforced central idea	E G A F P		
Vivid ending	E G A F P		

What did the speaker do most effectively? _____

What should the speaker pay special attention to next time? _____

General Comments: _____